CONTENTS

ACKNOWLEDGEMENTS

I would like to thank Christine Otter, Isabel Lim and Roxanne Rose for help with research. Many thanks to Professor Adrian Woods, of Brunel, for assistance with the research process. Gratitude is also due to Carol Saunders for help with the text, Philippa Poole for time and the Forte Foundation for financial assistance with the research.

INTRODUCTION

Sometimes the hospitality industry appears to have an essentially timeless quality that transcends the technology it uses. Certainly, technology has not transformed the hospitality industry in the same way that the manufacturing industry, financial services or even the armed services have been transformed.

The background to this book is research that I have conducted into information technology in the hospitality industry. Over a number of years I've looked at the industry and its use of information technology and I've been struck by the low take-up of computers. Where they are being used, I've been struck by how the reality of their use differs from the reasons given for their use. I've also been struck by the widely differing degrees of success that similar systems meet.

Although the industry and its technologists have been focused on the machines and their technical details, the minutiae of the technology seem to me to be a minor consideration in the application and 'success' of a system. What seems to be more important are the perceptions and actions of the people implementing the new systems.

Consequently, this is not a book focused primarily on the technology. There is no cut-away diagram of a floppy disc nor flow charts of possible hardware configurations. What I am looking at is less the 'how do you?' questions and more the 'why?' questions. Underlying every 'how?' are assumptions which shape the task and the way that a person wants to perform it. These assumptions (e.g. that information technology should speed up food service) are often seen as self-evident, but in reality are constantly changing and vary from one group to another. Do the food servers want a faster service? Does the customer want a faster service? If a faster service leads to significant customer resistance, does the manager want a faster service?

Previous books in this area take a standard approach, dividing up the subject matter by function. In this way, after a chapter on 'what is a computer?', chapters on hotel applications are followed by chapters on restaurant applications. This may be concluded with a chapter on choosing the right computer or computer system.

This books adopts a different approach and divides up the subject area into categories of users. It is the interaction between customers, operatives and management which decides what application and how it is to be used.

The equipment is just one part of technology. The people who use the hardware, and what they decide to do with it, are at least as important as the equipment and software itself. The equipment can be seen as plumbing, with information as the liquid that flows through the pipes. Sometimes this information is needed, sometimes it is used, sometimes it fails to flow, sometimes it is just effluent.

In 1982, the Hotel and Catering Industry Training Board produced a booklet advising hospitality managers on the introduction of computers. It had 11 pages on hardware, eight on software and three on 'the human factor'. This is a book primarily about the human factor. In my view it is the most important part of the process.

It's about communication between people. The rest is technology.
(Lars Ramqvist, head of Ericsson telecommunications company)

MARTIN PEACOCK
1995

1

Change: Unravelling the Process

Technology dominates our age. From our comedians to our politicians, from our college lecturers to our kitchen porters, one of the few things that we can agree on is its increasing importance. Yet while the term is bandied around, it loses any specific meaning and becomes one of those words whose shared meaning is assumed as its real meaning becomes obscure. Even my computerized grammar checker calls my 'cutting edge of technology' phrase a cliché and tells me not to use it. And, after all, it should know.

There is no doubt that information technology is effecting a profound change in all areas of our lives. The hospitality industry too is slowly being transformed through the application of advanced technological innovations, and this transformation is something more radical than mere improvements in machines. Technology, and more specifically information technology, needs to be put into its industrial and social context for its full significance to be understood.

The beginning of this chapter looks at what technology means, before going on to look at what factors influence it. Then, it explores the way in which technological change takes place: innovation. Finally, what makes 'information technology' so radically different from the preceding levels of technology is examined.

The term 'technology', 'the practical or industrial art(s)' (*Oxford Dictionary*), has three distinct aspects to its meaning. First, technology is the artefact or machine itself. Here technology means the physical reality: those things that you can touch, which help you to do your job. 'Things you can touch' are the hardware in computer terms: the monitors, printers, keyboards, etc. However an artefact, as a product of humans, also includes the software: electronic code that stores and can handle information. Software may be impossible to touch, but it is at least as important a consideration as hardware.

Second, technology consists of the skills or knowledge that enable you to use those machines or pieces of equipment. At a basic level this could be learning how to operate the keyboard: learning the rather crucial difference between the letter 'O' and the number '0'. At a higher level it would include the skills needed to design a system to achieve a business aim.

There is also a third side to the meaning of technology, one that is often neglected and is just as important as the previous two dimensions. This is the organizational context of the use of the machine, the power relationships that decide how we use that piece of equipment and that skill.

So, looking at a pen, the technology would be the pen itself, the skill that enables you to use it (i.e. writing), as well as the use to which it is being put. Is it being used to take notes? Why? If you wanted to study the pen, you could not separate the physical reality of the pen from the use people make of it.

This tripartite division of technology – artefact/skill/context – is just as important when you look at a large multinational hotel company. To begin with head office may decide to buy the machines and just dump them on an individual hotel: not as impossible a situation as you might think. Then it may realize that the staff need training on these machines, and so the staff are trained.

However, trained staff and machines that work do not necessarily produce a system that does what was intended. In one hotel this technology could be a riotous success, in another it could bomb disastrously. Staff motivation, supervision, the personal agendas of key players in this scenario must be looked at. Only when the three parts of technology are operating in harmony does a system 'work'.

MODELS OF TECHNOLOGY

Technology cannot be separated from society. What determines its impact? Which factors decide what becomes 'technology'? Only in looking at how society relates to technology can you learn how technology works at the micro level. Several models have been developed to attempt to explain its relationship to the various external factors.

The simplest is the idea that technology is just the product of innovative ideas that are then applied where appropriate by an industry. If a company is late in its application of appropriate technology, or uses the wrong technology, it loses its competitive advantage and ultimately goes bankrupt. This vision of people in white coats making scientific breakthroughs, and an attentive industry, is one beloved by the media and electioneering parties. It is an image of technology that can bring unease to a European industrialist when it is combined with another word to make the phrase '*Japanese* Technology'.

In its extreme form – 'technological determinism' – this model suggests that human activity is itself a product of the level reached by technology. It has been argued (Keegan, 1993), for example, that countries developed because they needed relatively disciplined armies for the close quarter battles that followed the development of metal weapons. If battles were fought with wooden spears and bows and arrows then they tended to be desultory, long-distance, individual affairs, with no need for elaborate authoritarian structures. Technology, in this case metal weapons, is claimed as the creator of the concept of country or kingdom.

This may seem a little far removed from our modern hospitality industry, yet most of the managers I have been in contact with during my research subscribe to a form of technological determinism. They see technology as something to be developed externally through its own separate processes. It then becomes the job of the hospitality manager to implement the technology, and eagerly (or not) to await the next development.

This model of technology can be taken a step further in contingency theory. This, now largely outmoded, theory suggested that technological innovations also determine the form of organization that a company uses. An emphasis on capital-intensive heavy machinery would lead to an emphasis on the conveyor-belt type of production, with mechanistic forms of control. Operatives would become automatons specializing in filling cardboard chip containers (for example), because that was the nature of the computerized deep fryer, combined with the sheer volume of chips to be packaged.

With this theory the type of organization used is seen simply as a product of the level of technology usage. Technology is seen as an independent process with its own inexorable force. This force is perceived as transcending not just the individual organization, but sometimes society itself.

Yet clichés like 'necessity (or laziness) is the mother of invention' merely point to how technological development is a process directed by people at both a conscious and unconscious level. Our information technology revolution owes a considerable debt to the American desire to put an American on the moon (and bring him back). It has been suggested that the American desire to reduce the weight of their electronic equipment has something to do with the particular German rocket scientists the Americans managed to capture at the end of the Second World War. That is, American rockets were under-powered (in comparison to the Soviet ones) and so there was an emphasis on reducing weight in their rockets. Certainly the relationship between the technology used by the hospitality industry today, and Cold War American military research is a subtle and complex one.

Technological development itself is a process subject to the objectives of the developers and their paymasters. It is not simply the outcome of a group of disinterested scientists seeking to expand the boundaries of human knowledge. However, just as important as technological development, is the *adoption* of technological innovations – a process mediated through a whole range of cultural factors.

As an illustration of this, possibly the most significant technological innovation in history was the development of gunpowder. For centuries the principal use the Chinese had for gunpowder was fireworks. In Japan, after the devastating effects of gunpowder had transformed the Japanese power structure at the battle of Nagashino (1575), the Japanese simply decided that it was no longer to be used. While the West was wrestling with the implications of any peasant being able to blow away privileged figures of authority who had spent their adult lives honing martial skills, the Japanese simply decided that the egalitarian consequences of firearms were simply too disruptive (Keegan, 1993). Only in 1854 were firearms reintroduced in significant numbers.

What happens to a technological innovation like gunpowder or a point of sales device, depends on the people who are introducing it. In the hospitality industry a specific innovation can be sold as the inevitable, natural, progressive option. What makes it so is not the innovation itself, but the perceptions of its users.

BREAKING DOWN THE INNOVATION PROCESS

To examine the transforming power of technology, it is necessary to look in detail at the process of innovation. Innovation is more than increasing levels of technological sophistication, yet technology is transmitted through the process of innovation. It is the lifeblood of commercial enterprises. A company that doesn't change, stagnates and, sooner or later, dies. Even companies which rely on an image of tradition are constantly changing behind the scenes. Clichés contain kernels of truth, and the only certainty in business (apart from taxation) is change, and an increasing rate of change at that.

The simplest breakdown of the process of innovation is: having the idea; developing it into a reality; and then implementing it in the market – i.e. creation, development and implementation. In a traditional manufacturing industry this division of an innovation could correspond to a company's divisional structure – a research and development department, leading to perhaps a design department, then an engineering department, a production department or factory and then to a marketing and sales department.

The Idea

Taking the creating or envisaging first, this could operate at a number of different levels. First there are individuals: creative people. In some companies these people are seen as complainers or dissidents, running against prevailing orthodoxies. 'Entrepreneurial' people can be a boon or a pain to a company whatever the corporate philosophy.

However, in a large, rigid, highly centralized company, people who argue for change are more likely to be seen as disruptive and a nuisance. Innovation entails risk: the possibility of money wasted, time misspent, humiliation at a corporate, departmental or individual level. When people can build careers on waiting for other people's mistakes it takes courage for a company to encourage risk-taking, and not automatically to punish failure. The acid test of a company's attitude to innovation is the career strategies of its staff: 'play safe, avoid change' or 'I believe in this, let's take a chance.'

The hospitality industry is not known for innovatory companies. Research and development departments are conspicuous by their absence. Corporate culture does not favour innovatory managers, and in large companies change is imposed from head offices. At these head offices accountants have a considerable influence in new developments, which tend to emphasize control and calculability rather than creativity. The term 'creative accountant' carries with it subtle pejorative connotations.

So where do the new ideas come from if not from within the industry? The hospitality industry uses outside companies which specialize in technological development. Research and development is an expensive, risky, capital-intensive business, and with the exception of the large fast-food chains, very little is conducted in-house. Even when large hotel companies claim their own badged products, they are usually bought from external consultancies.

The outside companies use trade fairs and advertising in the trade press to make hospitality companies aware of their products and services. To a large extent the trade press and trade fairs exist and are funded by these innovatory bodies.

This reliance on outside bodies produces its own tensions. In the hospitality industry a lot of currently used products were originally developed for the retail industry – and it shows. The licensed retailing sector has also seen its products overflow into the hotel and catering sector. If your main market is pubs, your food and drink management program can be altered, rebadged and sold to other parts of the hospitality sector. If the main initial cost was software development (all those highly paid programmers), this approach has advantages for the vendor.

Apart from outside companies, creativity in industry is also a product of companies monitoring their competitors. As a practice this is surprisingly rare for the hospitality industry, and there is little in the way of systematic monitoring of the competition. There is, however, some evidence of co-operation, for example where systems managers of large London hotels meet monthly as members of the Systems Managers' Association to demonstrate their new applications.

Another source of ideas comes about through the high turnover of staff, which is endemic in the hospitality industry. Constantly changing management brings with it a series of problems, but one advantage is that the manager has an appreciation of what a large number of establishments are using. The system you are familiar with can appear on your CV and be a factor in management selection.

So this 'envisaging' or creativity occurs at several different levels. At industry level, the hospitality sector imports wholesale from other industries, through the mechanism of the companies supplying the hardware and software. At company level, lack of scanning leads to a form of inertia. While at individual level, creativity is a response to the culture of the individual company, which on the whole does not smile at risk-taking.

The Development

The idea may be the beginning, but converting it into a practical proposition is a different stage. Very few systems can be bought 'off the peg' and simply installed on the companies' own computers. First the system needs to be configured for the company's hardware, or the hardware bought. More importantly, a simple installation needs decisions about who is to have access to what information, for example, what reports are required, and by whom? Modern systems come with a range of options of which only a few may be needed by the company. Superfluous options need to be removed. These are important decisions which need to be taken before the system is operating, and this is before the software vendors write new code to configure their application to the specific needs of the purchasers: 'bespoke' applications. Over half of the installations of modern, branded hospitality systems involve some element of tailoring to meet the specific needs of the client.

Crucial to this stage is the role of the 'expert'. With information technology there is a heavy reliance on self-styled 'solution houses'. These are the companies supplying the software and hardware. In a large number of cases the project can be simply handed over to the solutions house. The problem with this approach is that in a large number of cases the client company can simply abdicate responsibility and merely await the 'solutions at your fingertips' (Hotech '92 catalogue headline) – or not.

Hospitality system vendors make great play of the fact that they are hospitality-driven, rather than technology-driven. Their installers and salespeople tend to come from a hospitality industry background, rather than a computing one. With this background they are able to appreciate the language and problems of the hospitality industry and are able to respond sympathetically. (They also tend to be cheaper.)

'Contracting out' of the development of IT projects is where outside specialists are brought in to supervise and take responsibility. It is an increasingly common feature of the industry. In part 'contracting out' reflects a lack of self-confidence on the part of the client company. Nobody is suggesting that hospitality establishments should install a brand new system on their own, but the best system developments work as a partnership between client and vendor.

The installation of a new computer system is often portrayed (especially by vendors) as predominantly a technical exercise requiring specialist expertise. This can be accepted by line management who may feel they lack the necessary technical competence. However, most decisions taken during the installation of a project involve management functions rather than purely technical ones. For example, 'what type of cabling should we use?' appears a basically technical question, but to make this decision you need to know the future plans of the company. Perhaps in the future we are going to link guests to our system so that they can check their bill and order services from their room? How much information is going to be sent down these cables? How do we want to exchange information with head office? Something as seemingly mundane as cabling becomes an area where the management needs to be aware of the complexities of the issue and relate business plans to it. The artificial divide of technical versus managerial can hinder the relationship between a new management information system and corporate objectives.

Another interesting area in the development of a project is the pilot study. With a chain of establishments senior managers often decide to run the system in one outlet as an experiment. Sometimes the company will run more than one system in different outlets to compare the results.

Unfortunately, success in a pilot study does not automatically mean success in other outlets. Quite often the site for the pilot study is untypical in that ambitious managers may volunteer to have the study conducted in their outlet. They then have a vested interest in making the system work, which does not necessarily translate to other outlets. Management co-operation is crucial in the successful operation of any information system. Success is defined here not as the ability to send head office the reports it requires, but as the ability to manage a local unit more effectively.

We have seen how an idea might be applied to its industrial context and some of the pitfalls that can befall it. However, a successfully developed concept still has the main and most expensive hurdle still to cross.

The Implementation

One often neglected aspect of innovation is that any change at the workplace can bring about a positive effect. The Hawthorne effect, based on American experiments in the 1920s and 1930s, suggested that even attention alone (in this case from researchers) can improve productivity. These experiments have been criticized, especially for not taking sufficient account of changes in supervision. However, the fact remains that it is possible for *any* change to improve productivity, merely by overcoming feelings of neglect in the target group of workers. Innovation in itself, regardless of what it is supposed to achieve, can bring about the most surprising results.

Vendors of food and beverage control systems often claim savings of approximately five per cent in decreased wastage, such as pilfering. Remanco, a hospitality systems vendor, has claimed that its systems are 'often increasing profits by up to 6 per cent'. However, it is unrealistic to subscribe this entirely to the new system. First, merely announcing a new system has an effect on wastage. Pilfering is a (to some extent) tolerated, endemic feature of our industry. By flagging it as something that is going to be controlled it will be reduced.

Another reason why you can't use a 'before and after' approach to the costing of the benefits of a new system is the role of 'habit'. Within an industry not noted for its love of change, procedures can be the product not of rational decisions but of time. Long-forgotten results of battles between departments/individuals can be sanctified in time, and a love of routine keeps these procedures going. An individual may feel that this is not the best way of performing their task (a very common feeling in the hospitality industry), but that does not necessarily mean that they wish to change. This is what Weber termed the 'irrationality of bureaucracy'. People get attached to their working relationships, offices, even potted plants.

Once a new computer system is suggested, people question their previous routines and more rational procedures are developed. Often this can take place before the new system is implemented and increases in productivity ascribed to the computer system by managers attempting to justify the expenditure may actually have occurred before the installation. As an illustration, it is possible to reduce levels of pilfering in a restaurant simply by proposing a food and beverage control system.

Probably the biggest problem associated with innovation is not the envisaging or the development but *exnovation*. This means getting rid of old practices and is when the previously discussed inertia becomes resistance. One example of this is the battle of computer sizes. In the past, large companies had data processing departments that controlled large and expensive mainframes. These departments had almost a religious side, as white-coated minions administered to the needs of their god: the central computer. The advent of the microcomputer changed that, but the battle to remove the power of the centralized data processing department has taken the last decade to win.

Hypothetically, let's suggest that there is a feeling in a hospitality company that the current computer system is outdated. There is usually a choice of upgrading the present system or purchasing a new one. Upgrading usually has significant advantages, apart from being cheaper. First, the using department has built up a relationship with the initial vendor. Assuming the system has been successful, this department knows the system and has developed its own method of working, which it is unwilling to change.

A newly-developed system tends to have more facilities and advantages than an upgrade of an older system. You can keep on adding to an old program, but the joins will show. Within the company there will be a dispute over the two options and their relative merits. However, the crucial decider is unlikely to be purely 'objective' considerations, it is more likely to be the balance of power between the various departments. A new system might be bought if the using department loses out in a power struggle between various departments. The usual example in the hospitality industry is the food and beverage department losing out to accounts.

I know a consultant specializing in writing staff manuals for information systems, who describes the process as a political minefield. One thing a manual cannot do is tread on the political agendas of heads of departments. The system will almost certainly have been bought against the advice of some of these departmental heads and a few might be desperate for the system to fail.

Another major problem for a systems manual is to make it non-threatening to staff, especially those who have been in the job a long time. A manual has to stress the existing knowledge of operatives, sympathize about their workload ('amazing how you've managed to cope so far') and stress how the system is going to help them do their jobs.

A manual should not begin with an overview of the system, as this is too threatening. Instead it has to start with the micro: the operatives' own jobs, and proceed from there to the macro. A manual has to offer good, simple, unpatronizing advice, while stressing the tried and tested aspect of the system. Words that should not be used include 'rationalize' and 'efficiency'. 'Rationalize' implies the previous system was irrational and possible job losses. 'Efficiency' also has political overtones of job cuts, especially in the public services.

The Aftermath

Of course the installation is just the beginning. To make the system work there needs to be a commitment to training which the better vendors incorporate in their price. We'll look in detail at this process in later chapters.

Technological innovation: revolution or process?

Most people, when they think of innovation, think in terms of blinding flashes of inspiration leading to a completely new direction. This vision of change is one fostered by journalists in their search for copy and our own western culture. We have an individualistic culture which sees particular innovators as promoting revolutionary transformations: Whittle and the jet engine, Galileo and the telescope, etc.

Only God can create from nothing.
(Overheard conversation on a bus)

In reality innovation is a process rather than a specific event. The *idea/development/implementation* breakdown understates the complexity of the issues: at each stage other stages will be taking place. Although innovations can have a particular individual or company pinned on them, these innovations are the cumulative product of a series of minor developments and accidents. A computerized stock control system with hand-held terminals represents the products of a series of incremental steps. Some of these necessary steps came about before computers, for example the improvements in paper stock control pioneered in this country by Marks & Spencer.

Japanese culture is usually associated with successful technological innovation, yet that culture sees innovation as a slow, incremental process. A lot of stress is laid on minute improvements, with new products or services seen as reconstructed old ones. This is one of the reasons why Japanese management lays so much stress on staff suggestions, as part of the process of continuous improvement.

How we perceive innovation – process or revolution – can actually affect the process itself. Hospitality managers who see the introduction of computers as a global transformation of their business, rather than as an incremental step in the quest for greater efficiency, create a whole new series of problems for themselves.

WHAT IS INFORMATION TECHNOLOGY?

Technology and innovation have been with us since before we became human. Other primates use simple tools. What brings technological innovation to the fore is the development of information technology. If the Industrial Revolution left the hospitality industry relatively unscathed (in comparison with other industries), the transformations brought about through information technology will have far more dramatic effects.

If you define information technology as an artefact that can store information, then probably the first example is the abacus which was probably a simple refinement on the piles of stones used by ancient Greeks for their votes. Information technology is usually associated with the electronic storage and retrieval of information. The first machines with this facility were huge valve-driven machines that would occupy a large room.

It was the advent of the microprocessor and the silicon chip which significantly transformed this technology. With the ability to reliably store and process increasingly vast amounts of information, while taking up decreasing amounts of space, these tiny artefacts created the IT revolution.

Information technology as a term embraces all applications of these microprocessors and this is a wider term than simply computing. A computer is commonly associated with a specific piece of equipment, with a minimal set-up of monitor, central processing unit and a keyboard. However, microprocessors can be used in a range of equipment which is part of information technology, yet not usually defined as a computer, e.g. an electronic, hand-held, order-taking device.

Throughout history we have developed more complex and more sophisticated machines. One innovation has led to the next and it is tempting to see information technology as simply the next level of development.

This view of the computer as a 'supercalculator' is common, but it underestimates the fundamental change that information technology represents. In the same sense that the advent of the 'spinning jenny' or steam hammer was the beginning of a revolutionary change in people's lives, information technology has been proclaimed as a new revolutionary epoch: the information revolution as opposed to the industrial.

The essence of information technology is the storage and retrieval of information. The microprocessor chip processes an unimaginable number of transactions. What in the previous century would take an army of clerks a long period and a vast amount of paper can now be carried out by one person sitting at a small box in a few seconds. It is true that talk of the 'paperless office' seems ironic to those aware of the vast quantity of paper a computer printer can spew out, but paper no longer becomes the principal means for the transfer of information.

It is not just in comparison with the Industrial Revolution that IT shines. There has been a tremendous transformation during the IT revolution itself. Between 1958 and 1980, for example, the time for one electronic operation fell by a factor of

80 million (Porter and Millar, 1985). And this is a process which is continuing. There was some computerization in the hospitality industry during the 1950s, but it did not appear significantly until the 1970s.

Information technology has a potential, almost human quality, which is explored in science fiction literature. Computer systems can beat chess grand masters, operate nuclear deterrents, fly passenger aircraft more safely than humans and correct our spelling. Yet at the same time each of these God-like skills needs a human intervention. The computer doesn't actually correct our spelling, it simply provides us with a range of possible alternatives from which we make our choice. This tension between the computer as controller or assistant (master or slave) is a strong feature in the application of information technology.

The technology of the Industrial Revolution carried with it a wealth of implications for industrial organization and practice. From Adam Smith, Taylor and Henry Ford, industrialization tends to lean towards specialization and economies of scale. The conveyor belt is the archetypal symbol of the effect of this level of technology.

Using the production of business letters as an illustration, it can be seen that each level of technology appears to be linked with its own method of operation. This is what Clark and Staunton (1989) term 'soft determinism'. Before the Industrial Revolution, letters were produced very slowly, by hand, by clerks. The machine that industrialized business letter writing was the typewriter. Large organizations had their own 'typing pool', which was a factory for the typewritten word. Even in hotels, letter production was (and usually still is) separated as a function.

The cheap microcomputer (micros) changed this. Letter producers were not concentrated in one location but attached more towards the source of their copy. Large typing pools are a thing of the past. The next development will be the source of business correspondence (managers) producing their own correspondence. They have their own micros, usually have a limited ability to type and are actually originating the source copy themselves. It makes sense for the managers to produce their own letters. 'The vice-president will learn to use a keyboard, and eventually he will become a pianist' (Zuboff, 1988).

In this illustration, each level of technology has a different form of organization to go with it. However, it is noticeable how an organizational form used in a previous time can 'carry over' to the new technology. McDonalds applied the principles of the manufacturing industry to the restaurant sector. Strong specialization of jobs, standardization of product, a stress on uniformity of outcome are hallmarks of the factory rather than the restaurant. McDonalds has been accused of automating the customer (Ritzer, 1993). Used in this way, information technology is an adjunct of the factory: it monitors, measures, predicts and controls. The purpose of McDonalds' extensive use of computers would be easily recognizable to Henry Ford.

But information technology has two distinct sides. On one side it is an automator: it can increasingly take over routinized tasks and perform them in a way which reduces the need for human intervention. A computerized deep fryer which lifts the chip pan when the chips are cooked is a good example of this. Standardization of output and a reduction of labour costs are key components of the 'computer as automator' concept, which is really an extension of the ideas of the Industrial Revolution.

Information technology also has a second side, which Zuboff (1988) calls the 'informator'. Here IT provides information in a manner and in quantities not previously available. This produces fundamental changes in the way a business works. A customer database may have an 'automated' side (sending out junk mail), but it also has an informating side, since that information can be accessed, analysed and used to restructure marketing or the business itself. This is the unique and revolutionary feature of information technology.

Information as a raw material does not require the same form of processing as (for example) sheet metal. Once you have decided what you want from the sheet metal the processing becomes a mindless process to be undertaken as cheaply as possible: i.e. 'substituting machines for human labor' (Porter and Millar, 1985) p.152. Information as a raw material needs evaluation, analysis, hypothesis and synthesis. Information can be subject to a vast number of inferences. For effective utilization it needs discussion, experimentation, speculation: what Zuboff calls a 'collegiate style of management'. It is this tension between the two applications of information technology that we will explore in later chapters.

CONCLUSION

It is difficult to provide glib, one-sentence definitions of key terms like technology and innovation. The use people make of terminology has an illustrative power. The term technology carries with it a wealth of associations. Its meaning has a hierarchy of significances, when one is usually assumed as self-evident. Information technology is not simply an extension of the Industrial Revolution, it creates its own transformation even while its developers are still perceiving the computer as a supercalculator.

How technology is perceived within the hospitality industry is one of the most fundamental determinants of its use and its success. You cannot separate an artefact from the perceptions of its users.

DISCUSSION TOPICS

How might a social scientist in the Industrial Revolution define technology, and how would the definition differ from today?

What is the mother of invention, and why is she a mother, not a father?

If the computer was an animal, what type of animal would it be? Compare and contrast different people's responses.

What would be the advantages and disadvantages of a large hospitality company having its own research and development department responsible for the creation, development and installation of all innovations?

Why did McDonalds 'automate the customer'?

2

Customers: Consuming Computers

It may seem odd to include a chapter on the relationship between consumers and the new technology, but in a variety of different ways consumers decide on what technology is adopted, how technology is distributed, its function and its presentation.

Homilies about the hospitality industry as the 'people industry' abound, but they do contain a kernel of truth. The contact between the consumer and the provider of hospitality service is direct and all-embracing. First it involves increasingly uncommon, face to face contact with the consumer. The products or services are also perceived as significant by the consumer. Compare consumer reaction to a clothing shop's failure to provide a garment in the right size with a restaurant's failing to provide a steak with the required degree of cooking. Every consumer has his or her own concept of quality of service and product. Food and lodging are part of our everyday existence and perceived shortcomings lead to possible complaints, which may in turn result in loss of business.

'Problems with customers' form a large part of the hospitality operative's work and a significant proportion of his or her manager's time. These problems usually take place in front of colleagues, superiors and other customers. Not only is your handling of these incidents used in your superior's evaluation of you, but they are stressful in themselves. How a waiter or waitress feels at the end of a shift can have more to do with the behaviour of customers than the physical workload.

Nurses deal with the stresses of their own jobs by developing formalized procedures to deal with client-related stress, such as when people die (Glaser and Strauss, 1967). In the same way, operatives in the hospitality industry seek to distance themselves from the stress of their direct contact with the client through procedures and rituals. From the Disneyland worker's scripted ad libs, to the rigmarole of opening a wine bottle in a high-status restaurant, operatives seek to alleviate the stress of spontaneous direct contact with the client.

At the same time, one of the things the client desires is exactly this personal contact: the sense of a name remembered, special demands being accommodated. A customer wants to feel like a unique individual human being, even in McDonalds. This tension between the consumer's demand for humanity and the industry's inability or unwillingness to respond lies at the heart of the modern hospitality industry. Apart from other considerations, human contact is expensive.

Management can sometimes define the search for business efficiency as an increasing volume of business with a reduction in the number of staff. There is a price on the friendly conversation between guest and member of staff. What price is the hospitality industry prepared to pay?

Some establishments can claim to treat their customers with respect and humanity. Some companies can fake it. Some don't even bother faking it. The crucial question remains: what does the customer want?

FACTORY OR WORKSHOP?

> *'What'd they call a Big Mac?'*
> *'Well, Big Mac's a Big Mac, but they call it "Le Big Mac"'*
> *'Le Big Mac. What do they call a Whopper?'*
> *'I dunno. I didn't go into a Burger King.'*
>
> *Pulp Fiction* (1994),
> Quentin Tarantino

Our age is often seen as the triumph of the single, monolithic hospitality company. With a simple, heavily marketed, strongly branded product, the internationally standardized company is sometimes perceived as sweeping all before it. The 'McDonalds in Moscow' syndrome can be perceived as the victory of a simple, uniform product.

To take McDonalds as our example of this type of business formula, it has more than 9,000 outlets worldwide, and it is the largest property owner in the United States. In a 1986 survey, 96 per cent of American children were able to identify Ronald McDonald, making him second only to Father Christmas in name recognition. Part of the reason for the McDonald brothers' initial success was their concentration (in 1948) on a very limited range of hamburgers and their great stress on the role of technology. McDonalds developed its own equipment, which was to be used in all its franchised outlets.

Great emphasis was put on maintaining the quality of the original concept. In the past, people who had bought franchises had watered down an originally successful concept, by such devices as buying cheaper ingredients in exchange for bribes. Ray Kroc, who was responsible for the expansion of the McDonalds franchises, successfully maintained the quality of his outlets. Kroc's own background lay with technology.

McDonalds was the application of factory methods of operations to the hospitality industry. There was an emphasis on volume of production, with relatively lower profit margins. Each job was broken down into its component tasks and carefully analysed and improved, with different people working to assemble the 'Big Mac'. The new approach to restaurant work was adopted based on 'pre-defined and tightly synchronised teamwork' (Clark and Staunton, 1989). Kroc was the Henry Ford of the hospitality industry, but his real success lies not in his automation of food production but in his automation of food consumption: automating the customer. 'That is, when customers enter the fast-food restaurant or wend their way along the drive-through, they enter a kind of automated system through which they are impelled and from which they are ultimately ejected when they are "refuelled" ' (Ritzer, 1993, p.156).

The spirit of the factory was also used in the application of information technology. McDonalds developed their own finely tuned systems of ordering and stock control, points of sales and staff management. These systems emphasized speed and central control. Ritzer sees the hallmark of the McDonalds systems as: efficiency, calculability, predictability and control. There's an irony in these; Kroc never produced a business plan or used a profit and loss statement in his life.

Today the McDonalds image of information technology has taken the hospitality industry by storm. Most hospitality managers, when asked for a successful application of IT in their industry tend to pick McDonalds. The only exception to this is McDonalds managers who have a tendency to pick Burger King (Peacock, 1994c). It is an image that carries the McDonalds ethos: strong, centralized control, vigorous standardization and an emphasis on volume of production.

Yet the McDonalds image of the future of the hospitality industry, with its concomitant use of information technology, is a vision that is increasingly being questioned. McDonalds is an organization under increasing pressure, in the USA its profit margins are down and the queues in Moscow no longer stretch around the square. We are seeing the emergence of a different type of consumer: more sophisticated, fickle, fashion-conscious and differentiated. What the consumer is increasingly interested in is a unique quality. Consumption patterns have become an expression of difference rather than similarities. The shopping mall with its internationally recognized catering outlets is gradually being questioned by consumers, who are looking more to retail outlets which offer diversity and individuality. This market segmentation is an increasing feature of the affluent world, even if the USA is leading the trend.

To cynical consumers still eager to consume, the meal experience can represent the supreme commodity. It is a disposable, transient experience which subtly marks the consumer as a temporary member of some social sub-group, for example: 'We had Japanese last night'. In comparison to our ('this week's colour') Benetton sweater, the meal 'is not going to languish in a drawer long after the purchase has become an outmoded expression of the consumer's individuality' (Peacock, 1993b, p.303).

Consumption patterns like these do not fit the McDonalds model. Of course McDonalds can hit back by directing their marketing at the most unsophisticated consumers (children) and large multinationals can diversify and run small chains of simulated French bistros with fake fading wallpaper – but this approach is under pressure.

The erosion of large multinationals with a heavily branded product can be overstated. McDonalds is unlikely to stop expanding, and patterns of consumption are always related to levels of disposable income. Relatively wealthier consumers traditionally have more differentiated consumption patterns. Most consumers still like the certainty of a standard product and service behind the neon insignia. Mass marketing techniques have a tremendous power which is fully exploited by international hospitality enterprises. However, consumption patterns *are* changing and even mass marketing is having to target a more cynical and differentiated consumer.

To some extent the type of consumer varies with location. Some countries, such as France, are more resistant to the internationally branded product. Inside a country, the more cynical consumer is to be found more in the urban concentrations. Even within a major metropolitan conurbation like London, there is a shift towards the more unique eating establishment the nearer the consumer moves to the centre of the city. However what we are seeing is an incremental process, which will effect most consumers, not just fashion-conscious London consumers.

One name for this break down of the mass market is 'de-massification' (Crawford-Welch, 1993a) and it has a number of implications for the use of information technology. Most importantly, the increasing emphasis on flexibility and change does not fit the McDonald's model of information technology as a controlling medium. With the shift from standardization to diversification, information technology becomes more a tool of prediction rather than control. How the technology is used has a direct relationship to the type of market.

How does the computer effect the interaction between the consumer and the operative? We have looked at a shift in patterns of consumption and the possibility that this might impact on the use of information technology. It is now necessary to look at the way computers and consumers interact.

CUSTOMER MEETS THE COMPUTER

Information technology can be both de-humanizer and humanizer, depending on its context and application. The alienating effect of technology has been one of the cultural themes of the twentieth century and there are a whole range of responses that can be taken towards IT by the hospitality manager.

Information Technology as the Enemy of Customer Service

Case Study: Athenaeum Hotel

The Athenaeum Hotel, London, had a Yaletronics key card system. Now a common type of key system in medium to large hotels, with these systems the customer is given a plastic card which acts as a key to his or her room. The card is valid for that customer, and when the next customer arrives, they get a new and unique card. If the guest takes the card away, there is no problem, a new one can be produced. At the Athenaeum Hotel this system was replaced with a new Marlock system, with the cards replaced with traditional metal keys. These keys were handed in to reception when the guest left and had to be stored behind the desk. The motivation behind the change, was that it was felt that the original key cards did not fit the classical, luxury image that the hotel wanted to project. With Americans making up half the guests, the hotel wanted to promote an image of 'quaintness', and the traditional metal keys fitted that image.

There were a series of drawbacks to the new Marlock system. Apart from the initial installation costs, there were the cost of lost keys and the labour costs in storing and handling guest keys. Ironically the new key system has large plastic tabs indicating the room number, attached to the keys.

Although the new key system was chosen as a reaction against modern technology, the Marlock key system had some hidden sophistication. Unlocking the door would turn on the lights and air conditioning, thereby retaining some of the innovations which were brought in by systems like Yaletronics. It is also possible to link all the locks to a central computer.

Here, information technology, as represented by the key cards, was seen as a threat to their conception of service. A considerable amount of money was spent trying to establish a more traditional image. Ironically the new system was potentially at least as sophisticated as the key card system. It was just that this was disguised with a veneer of old-fashioned charm.

The belief that information technology and customer service are opposites, used to be a strong feature of the hospitality industry. How can the 'human touch' and computer processing co-exist? The tension between the two in the minds of the hospitality manager can produce a whole range of responses.

This leads us to the next type of response to the new technology: the invisible assistant.

'Look no Computers'

Case Study: The Lanesborough Hotel

Most people don't like the feeling of talking to computers. As a researcher, when I'm conducting telephone interviews, I find people less free with their answers when they can hear me typing their responses into a computer. Respondents can handle the yes/no responses but anything more was difficult. It's almost as if people feel as if 'anything you say could be used against you'.

In the same way, hotels have always attempted to minimize the impact of front-of-house computers, hiding them (if they could afford it) behind their mock mahogany desks. The Lanesborough Hotel, London, has taken this one stage further and put the front-of-house computers in another room.

The American-owned Lanesborough considers itself to be the best hotel in London and has a style reminiscent of an English stately home (apart from the bullet-proof windows). The sales literature of the company that supplied their software says that 'in reflecting the elegance of early 19th century residences, The Lanesborough promises to capture the charm of a bygone era'. Guests are not greeted at a traditional front desk but by armchairs and antique furniture. The customary front desk marks the psychological and physical barrier between the guest and smiling/grimacing reception staff. By removing the desk, the hotel has emphasized the personal and human touch. Guests are welcomed by name and the actual check-in occurs in the guest's room. Here the client signs the pre-printed registration card.

It can only do this for two reasons. First, it has a relatively small number of high-paying customers (95 rooms or suites). Second, it has a very sophisticated system hidden behind the scenes. This system can deal with a range of services, including sports scheduling (e.g. booking the guest a round of golf), limousine scheduling, guest safes, room movie systems, room honour bars. All of these services are dealt with by the computer system and appear directly (and itemized) on the guest's bill.

At the Lanesborough the customer is not aware of the system. It is hidden to enhance the quality of the service. Perversely, the quality of service would be poor, or even more expensively labour intensive, if it was not for the sophisticated system that is hidden from the guest.

The Lanesborough represents an expensive product, out of reach to all but an extreme minority of very wealthy, principally American, customers. Through recruitment and training, emphasis is placed on the quality of the interaction between guest and member of staff. It is an expensive choice. What happens if you decide to use the technology differently?

'Look no Humans!'

If human labour is expensive and hospitality managers equate business efficiency with a reduction in staff numbers, while maintaining some perception of 'quality', then the logical consequence is the automated hotel.

The technology exists at the moment. Automated check-ins can take your credit card details and provide you with a card key for your room. The front desk disappears again. Security is handled through the use of technology such as video cameras. Refreshments can be provided through a combination of in-room facilities (automated bar and/or a kettle and tea/coffee), and vending machines. Check-out can be automated, with your credit card automatically debited and an itemized receipt printed out at the hotel or posted on. Financial information on the performance of the hotel could simply be automatically downloaded to head office.

With the present level of technology this hotel would still need maintenance and cleaning staff, but only as long as these services are provided cheaper by humans than machines. Today even staffed public toilets are being replaced with highly expensive, automated, self-cleaning ones, because of the cost of cleaning staff.

The concept of the automated hotel causes most potential consumers to feel uneasy. In lots of ways it represents one end of the technological spectrum, whose approach is determined by consumer resistance. I still remember my wariness on entering my first automated toilet, complete with its piped James Bond theme music. But consumer resistance can be a temporary phenomenum, and sometimes lack of human interaction can increase the consumption of services.

In the past some hotels would have a telephone operator, who would provide you with a number or sometimes an outside line. When these telephonists were replaced by automated switchboards/call loggers (to reduce staff numbers) some hotels expected the use of telephones to go down. In fact the opposite occurred as guests found the absence of the switchboard operator less restricting on the use of the phone. They were embarrassed, or found it inconvenient, to use the operator.

Some people feel resistant towards hotels because of the fear of embarrassment. Hotel staff can have an impact on the potential guest which is not always positive and welcoming. As Jenny Wynne noted, the phrase 'Can I help you?' can carry a whole range of subtle intimidating implications such as, 'What are you doing here? You look out of your depth'. Hospitality enterprises can be minefields of social etiquette to some potential customers. A cheap automated service has a certain appeal, if only for the minimizing of the 'incongruent encounters' (Wynne, 1994).

To an extent what determines people's acceptance of advanced technology is what they are familiar with in the home. Relatively sophisticated room movie systems find acceptance because the consumer uses the equivalent video systems at home. Automated check-outs, used as a time-saving adjunct to the front office, are becoming more acceptable because of the use of ATM (cashpoint machines).

In Britain, acceptance of technological innovation has a class dimension. You can demonstrate this with the (unlikely) idea of a 'country house' hotel with a satellite dish displayed prominently on its frontage. New products and services find much more acceptance with affluent manual workers than they do with the professional middle classes or the upper classes. This is true whether they are 'drive-in' hamburger restaurants, video recorders or portable phones. Long-standing, high-class hotels in Europe sometimes give the impression that they have never quite got over their guests arriving in cars rather than carriages.

What you are paying for with money is often an increasing personal touch: other people devoting time to you. In class terms this could be the theatre instead of the cinema, the restaurant 'greeter' who can remember your name, instead of the anonymous voice barking at you in the drive-in hamburger restaurant, the cluster of servers at your table as opposed to the sandwich that comes from the vending machine. There is this tension between increasing affluence and increasing technology.

In a number of ways the automated hotel represents a rather dated image. It is part of an age which believed in the progressive, wealth-creating force of technology: the '*Tomorrow's World*' spectacle of new life-enhancing machines, that somehow never fulfilled their promise. McDonalds do not use images of their technology to sell their products, they use happy smiling faces of (alleged) members of staff or happy smiling symbolic figures.

Automated hospitality enterprises will become an increasing feature of the industry, particularly at the budget end of the market, but the main use of information technology will be in enhancing customer service, rather than replacing it. In this scenario, information technology is used to produce a personalized service. At its worst this will mean an increasing use of personally addressed junk mail, at its best it will mean a product or service tailored to the needs and wishes of the consumer.

The first stage of this process is finding out what the consumer wants. The Marriott chain in the USA conducted a large survey of its potential customers and, using various computerized statistical packages and conjoint analysis, produced a detailed specification of what their consumers wanted and what they were prepared to pay for. The result of this investigation was the 'Courtyard by Marriott' concept, which has achieved considerable success in the USA.

As well as ascertaining future consumer behaviour, information technology can be used to store and use past consumer behaviour: guest histories. One restaurant owner of my acquaintance, responds to every confident telephone booking with the statement: 'Ah! You have eaten here before.' He has a high proportion of repeat business, so if the customer has eaten there before he feels remembered, even though he or she isn't. The tactic does not offend new customers, but as an approach to customer services it lacks sophistication.

Modern systems store a considerable amount of information concerning a customer. As well as details of what he or she consumed, dates and address, payment methods and type of business are recorded as a matter of course. Possibly the most fundamental question is 'How did you hear about us?' In a well-organized hotel this information can be provided during the conversation with the person taking the guest to the room and then put into the system when the staff member returns. 'What attracted you to us?' is also a fundamental question.

The guest is unlikely to be remembered on a subsequent visit, but by entering the name on reservation, facts about any previous visits can be automatically put on the screen: the same room can be offered, requests can be anticipated and the customer's perception of the service is enhanced. Having said this, guest history represents an under-utilized feature of those hotels who are using a property management system. Even the well-computerized, large hotels rarely use their guest history system for anything other than basic sales leads. One well-respected hotel chain uses a paper form for its marketing system data collection, when the same information is already available on its computerized guest history. In the context of an increasingly competitive struggle for customers, guest histories represent an untapped gold mine. As Crawford-Welch (1993a, p.107) notes: 'The competitive edge will not come from having information, rather it will come from how that information is used.'

As the industry becomes increasing consumer-oriented, rather than product- or service-centred, 'Database profiling will become the rule for catering to the needs and wants of the international consumer' Crawford-Welch (1993b, p.193). This will involve not just knowing your own consumers, but your competitor's consumers. After all, shouldn't they soon be yours?

Information provides a wealth of means for enhancing customer service. One imaginative use is as a measure for a medium of exchange. RCI's (Resort Condominiums International) business is based on people exchanging their timeshares with someone else's part share in a property. Despite image problems in this country, Timeshare is a significant part of the hospitality market. In this country hotels have been successfully converted into timeshare apartments.

A family might own a twenty-sixth of a Lake District villa, which gives them a fortnight a year. Bored with the Lake District they want a fortnight in somebody else's timeshare in Tuscany. Through the company they arrange a swop, but how do you make sure that the two properties are of equivalent value?

The solution is that every customer is given a detailed record to fill in about their holiday accommodation. Return rates for the questionnaire are high and the responses are fed into the computer where they are analysed and a measure is evolved for the quality of the accommodation. Here, information technology is being used to measure the quality of the product (accommodation) and this measure is an aggregation of the views of the people who have stayed there. The value of the apartment or villa is 'grounded' in the perception of the consumers.

Without the application of information technology it would be impossible to provide a sophisticated measure of the product and the end result would be an increase in consumer dissatisfaction and complaints. This is using information technology to enhance service.

CONCLUSION

The relationship between the consumer and the hospitality enterprise is a complex and multi-faceted one, mediated through a whole range of technological options. Information technology can be combined with a standardized and strongly branded product to produce a centrally directed and controlled service. In the factory analogy consumers become unit throughputs to be measured, manipulated and controlled. 'How many units did you shift?' can be room nights, or meal experiences.

Increasingly, consumers are reacting against this vision of customer service and their tastes are veering away from internationally standardized services. Information technology has an enabling side which, imaginatively used, can enrich the experience of customers.

The spectrum of service quality does not run from the alienation of the automated inner-city hotel front desk to the customer-friendly, uncomputerized country hotel. Top class service may be inseparable from its (albeit discreet) information systems, as at the Lanesborough. If, today, the prejudices of hospitality managers and consumers can equate computers and consumer-unfriendliness, then within decades prejudices will be working the other way round, and we might see the emergence of the dummy computer for that consumer-friendly look.

DISCUSSION TOPICS

Is the hospitality industry more stressful to work in than other industries? If so, what makes it so?

The original McDonalds was centred around a barbecue pit. Could the current McDonalds do this?

Does the student market show signs of 'de-massification'?

What does 'quaintness' as a marketing ploy mean for information technology?

What type of customer might favour an automated hotel?

3

Operatives: The Quest for 'Something Different' and Backdoor Empowerment

While customers provide the target and focus of a business and its associated information technology, the people that come into most contact with IT are the staff or operatives. Rarely are their reactions or responses analysed, yet the transformations in their jobs are fundamental and far-reaching. This chapter looks at the relationship between the operatives and their technology, using evidence from British industry.

One of the most enduring myths about British industry is the story of widespread worker resistance to technological change. It is difficult to see the origin of this myth. Certainly, the search for scapegoats for Britain's relative industrial decline plays a part, and newspaper portrayals of the struggle between print unions and newspaper owners have had a hand. However it is still difficult to find reasons why this myth is believed by many sections of British industry.

The reality is that the majority of British workers positively welcome technological change. Commenting on the widest survey of attitudes to new technology, Daniel (1987, p.260) stated that contrary to conventional wisdom 'British workers generally experience and accept a very high level of major change'. He noted strong resistance to advanced technological change (i.e. computerization) in only one in 50 establishments and such was the widespread support from operatives that 'managements have not had to use consultation, participation or negotiation to win their consent to change'.

Table 3.1 Staff views towards a new system

	Before installation	After installation
Happy/positive	56%	74%
Apprehensive/negative	18%	13%
Mixed/neutral	26%	13%

Source: Peacock, (1994c)

In the hospitality industry this picture is repeated. A 1994 survey of staff attitudes in over 200 establishments found widespread acceptance of new systems when they were suggested, which became even more favourable after installation, as shown in Table 3.1.

These figures came from managers' own assessments of staff views and there is some evidence to suggest that they overemphasized negative reactions. Certainly, managers who believed that staff would oppose change were characterized by the fact that they had not talked to their staff. Negative feelings from staff after installation tended to be linked to technical problems connected with the new system itself.

What is more remarkable about these figures is the background to the positive feelings. There is no evidence of the involvement of human resource managers in this process of change. In fewer than one in five establishments were the staff talked to about the proposed changes, let alone any formal consultation. In one large hotel, part of a chain that 'puts people first', the manager commented that 'staff were not an issue'.

Managers tended to believe that the positive feelings of their staff were untypical of the industry and reflected the individual characteristics of the establishment: 'We've got a good bunch here.' However it was precisely because the positive feelings towards computerization were so general among staff that management could successfully impose dramatic changes with so little consultation and negotiation.

The Luddites

Only at one point in this country has there been significant opposition to technological developments from operatives, and this was outside living memory (1812). Croppers were a group of male workers who used oversized garden shears to cut the furry parts off the surface of new cloth. This was a major economic activity carried out in independent workshops in the north of England. The work was physically demanding and the croppers tended to be very strong young men, who were also exceptionally well-paid.

A machine was developed that would replace them and with the economy declining there was systematic resistance. Large bodies of men, acting in well-organized armed bands, systematically destroyed these machines and intimidated the owners who were introducing the machines. They named themselves (ironically) after an apprentice who had smashed the machines of his workplace in a fit of temper: Ludd.

At first these Luddites were astonishingly successful. They had the support of a considerable portion of the population, and were opposing their loss of earnings and the general economic harm which they felt a factory system would bring about.

Initially the Luddites met with no opposition on their nightly excursions, but the government was soon forced to act. A huge military presence was drafted into the north of England, large numbers of spies were introduced and suspects were tortured for information. All of this, combined with a law against secret oaths (which held the Luddites together) and a lack of leadership from within the Luddite movement, eventually led to their destruction.

The alleged leaders were given a mass execution near York Castle in front of a huge, silent, sympathetic crowd, after a trial that can only be described as suspect. Their bodies were sent for dissection so that their graves did not become symbols of resistance.

So what is the relevance of the Luddites for the hospitality industry? One of the factors determining our culture is our history. If, as a country, we have an exceptionally tolerant attitude towards the effects of technological change, then one of the long-distant causes for this is what happened to the Luddites. If the Luddites had won – which was possible (Reid, 1986) – then this country's attitude towards technological change now might be totally different.

Technophobia

Technophobia is a morbid fear of, or aversion to, machines, or more specifically computers. It is usually a reflection of a person's sense of inadequacy when faced with a new, complex piece of equipment. Symptoms include a reluctance to use the computer, an undue reliance on inflexible instructions, usually in the form of a post-it note stuck to the monitor, and extreme responses to problems, sometimes coupled with an inability to read the instructions on the screen.

High levels of technophobia are popularly associated with increasing age, as children today tend to overcome their technophobia around the age of six. Statements like: 'My seven-year-old nephew could handle this, but I never will' are classical symptoms.

In extreme cases patients tend to anthropomorphize the computer, giving it a name (usually of the opposite sex) and a demonic character. In these cases the computer-caused frustrations are seen as the computer deliberately obstructing the work of the operator.

The cure is a course of training which emphasizes the computer as a dumb box of wires, awaiting your instructions. Increasing emphasis on graphical user interfaces where the software is arranged more as pictures, with a mouse that can be moved and clicked on the required task, greatly simplify this process. Software design increasingly stresses 'user-friendliness', which minimizes the adjustment period. Technophobia is a normal process which everyone goes through, even if they have subsequently forgotten it. If the phobia persists, the fault tends to lie in the training rather than the individual.

Technophilia

Technophilia is a love of machines, or more specifically an undue love of computers. An increasing phenomenon, it is usually (but not exclusively) a male characteristic. Computer problems can be engrossing and, rather like crosswords, some people, colloquially known as techies (pronounced tekkies), can find them all-absorbing and challenging. All organizations need at least one person who looks at computers like this. However, a problem develops if this person devotes him or herself to issues which bear no relationship to the priorities of the business.

A minor symptom can be a love of computer games, which although an innocuous pursuit in itself, can be a costly business in terms of company time, or even in terms of telephone bills for games which are interactive. Games can be both addictive and contagious. Modern games sometimes come with a realistic spreadsheet, which can be activated at the press of a button when supervision is near.

Technophilia is also associated with a love of the most up-to-date hardware. There is always a piece of hardware which is faster, smaller, more modern looking, but technophiliacs must not be given unchecked power over purchasing. Some companies can exhibit technophiliac tendencies, but I am not aware of any in the hospitality industry. *There is no cure, all you can do is isolate and contain.*

Of course attitudes to computers vary with the individual. There are technophobics who do their best to refuse to have anything to do with computers. However, the popularity of the assumption that this mainly consists of mature individuals needs to be challenged. There is no evidence that age is a barrier to effective use of IT. Although an older person may begin with a greater technophobia, with good training this disappears. One interviewed software vendor suggested that because older people had seen more dramatic changes during the course of their lives he felt that they were more open to the prospect of change.

One area where there is considerable resistance to change is organizational restructuring, and this is true for all of British industry. Where jobs are redefined, departments restructured, environments altered or staff relocated there is widespread unhappiness and resistance. In part this is related to fears of a drop in pay or redundancy, but it is more than this. A computerization with possible job losses will be more popular than organizational change which carries guarantees against job losses. People are simply happier with the prospect of changing technology than they are with the prospect of changing people.

Staff who have been in a job for a period of years or decades, who also tend to be older, are those most resistant to organizational change. They have built up patterns of work which they are reluctant to alter. Of course technological change and organizational change are related, and in fact (as will be argued later) should be related. But, in terms of their impact on the workforce, they should be treated as two distinct issues.

POPULARITY RATIONALE

Why is technological change so popular with operatives? It is certainly not because of the care that management takes in selling a package to its workforce. It is certainly not because workers' views are taken into account when tailoring a package to a particular workplace. Implementation gives no sense of empowerment to hospitality workers, rather it tends to underline their marginal significance in the eyes of hospitality managers.

First, operatives generally find their work more interesting. A survey of hospitality operatives (Peacock, 1994c) found that over two-thirds found their work more stimulating after computerization, while most of the rest noted no change. This is a more favourable response than Daniel's survey of office workers. As an old system is replaced with a newer one, that too appears to make the work more interesting. More modern systems have a greater speed, flexibility and range of facilities and these are favoured by the hospitality operative.

In interviews, hospitality managers would often express surprise at the way in which operatives would acquire information from parts of the system not directly connected with their jobs. This is at a time when considerable effort is being put into restricting information to 'authorized' eyes only. While it is not a good idea to give general access to maintenance functions (e.g. let anyone change all the passwords), often the more open the system, the more sophisticated it is.

A second reason for the popularity of IT among hospitality operatives is that skill levels are greater. Again, managers claimed over two-thirds of operatives had higher levels of skill, with most of those remaining seeing no change. This is also a more significant change than detected among office workers. A new computer system does not just bring with it skills in IT, but also appears to affect the job content itself. More judgements are required by operatives and the operatives favour this.

Almost half of hospitality operatives feel that their new computer system gives them more responsibility, while a third feels that it makes no real difference. Again, comparing this to Daniel's survey of office workers, the hospitality industry is seeing a more marked change. The skilled judgements which an operative is increasingly called upon to make, involve taking increasingly important decisions and, while there are operatives who don't want extra responsibility, most find this a positive step forward.

Almost six out of ten workers in hotels and restaurants find that new systems have meant less supervision and more control over how they do their own job. This is twice the proportion of office workers. Of the four other workers, two in every ten have noted no change while two find less control and more supervision.

Autonomy at work is not something traditionally associated with the hospitality industry, yet the trends indicated above mark a significant change in the nature of work. At the moment, information technology has touched a small proportion of jobs in the industry. However, it is an increasing proportion and the rate of increase is accelerating.

'INFORMATING' THE WORKPLACE

The shift in responsibility and autonomy towards hospitality operatives with computers is the 'informating capability' of information technology, which I touched upon in Chapter 1. Basically, a computer can do 'mindless' work more effectively; it is quicker and so cheaper, but it is also more reliable. American Department of Defense studies show that the error rate in recording data through bar coding is one in 3 million, compared with one in 300 for manual data entries (quoted by Porter and Millar, 1985). As mindless tasks become computerized this leaves the 'mind' tasks: tasks requiring thought and analysis.

This process has been called 'textualization'. In the past operatives have been more concerned with reproducing text: following instructions, typing letters, putting data into another form. With an information system the data (ideally) is only entered once, and the operative is less concerned with entering data and more concerned with acting on it. A good property management system should be able to generate an address simply from typing in the postal code and house number. A Pizzahut pizza delivery system can produce customer details on the entry of a telephone number. This information can then be used for a variety of business-related purposes.

Transformations in the nature of work, brought about by information technology, can be seen clearly in other industries. For example, in the gas supply industry 20 years ago, organization was on a strongly segmented departmental basis. The work of operatives was largely the processing of written information. A customer contacting this type of organization could have an exceedingly frustrating time. They might be passed from one department to the next, and sometimes it would appear to the frustrated customer as if the main role of operatives was to determine how a problem was not their specific responsibility. Their strictly bureaucratic approach would mean following a set of regulations which gives a good illustration of the destructive effects of the 'work to rule'.

It was decided to change the approach to customer services using information technology. Information that was previously the privileged territory of departments would be made available to all. The customer would ring a 'one stop' number, and ideally the person answering would be able to deal with 95 per cent of problems or queries. Only in a minority of cases would the call be referred to specialists.

The end result was not only a transformation of customer relations, but also a transformation in the role of the operative. Personal skills and problem-solving (rather than passing) skills became all-important. Decisions become the province of the operative, who, backed by the management information system, can make informed judgements, which would previously have been made by supervisors.

This transformation of work is only just beginning in the hospitality industry but its potential can be illustrated. The Copthorne Tara is a large, 825-roomed, central London Hotel with a reasonable claim to have (in the words of a manager) 'the most up-to-date systems in the country . . . second to none'. Their reservations staff will usually be handling over £45,000 worth of business a day.

A crucial issue for any large hotel is overbooking. A hotel may be full in terms of promised customers, but any experienced hotelier realizes that a significant proportion of these bookings will cancel or 'not show' for a variety of reasons. If the hotel is just booked out until 'full', these 'no shows' will mean empty rooms and reduced revenues.

The solution is to overbook, but the question is, by how much? Reservations staff are characteristically reluctant to overbook. If too many customers do turn up, they will have to be sent to another hotel ('walk someone out of the hotel') and there is the possibility of a scene and a loss of goodwill. At the Copthorne Tara generally the staff were happy with an overbooking of 20–25, but their computer system was suggesting (based on its history of past events) around 45. This is an increase in revenue of around £2,000 a day, with only a minimal increase in the hotel's costs.

There are complications. This scenario only works when the hotel is fully booked and demand for hotel rooms is not controlled by the hotel. It varies with external factors such as disruptions to public transport and the weather. You also need to know what proportion of the bookings are 'guaranteed', that is, more likely to show, as more guaranteed rooms will reduce how much you overbook.

The fact remains that reservations staff, earning approximately £50 a day can make £2,000 a day difference to revenues by overbooking more carefully. Reservations at a large hotel are constantly changing, the person most informed about the current 'state of play' is the computer operative, and the crucial, revenue-influencing decisions are being taken more and more at this level. With the use of the technology available to them, reservations staff can reduce the number of empty beds and increase revenue, while not increasing the number of guests who have to be 'booked out' to another hotel.

Take the issue of price haggling. If a potential customer claims that a competitor hotel is offering the same service at a cheaper price, what should the hotel do? It is possible that a large hotel can be offering over a hundred different rates. The answer is that 'it depends'. It depends if the rival hotel is really offering that price point, on the current level of bookings, on anticipated levels of demand for each price point on the requested day. The first five words that the operative uses in response to the price query will make or break the sale. For maximum business effectiveness the decision needs to made at the operative level.

It is psychologically difficult for reservation staff to push the higher rates. A £120 room sounds expensive to someone earning £50 a day who does not habitually stay in hotels. But 'upselling' and extracting the maximum available rate for the room are ways in which a hotel can significantly increase its revenue, while not greatly increasing costs. To maximize revenue it is important that the decision-making capability is located in the operative and that this operative has the information technology to help them make the best decision.

This type of role for reservations staff is being resisted throughout the industry. It involves a shift in power which, although taking place gradually, is rarely the product of a conscious decision. One reason for this is the way in which reservations staff are perceived. Reservations staff are predominantly female and their managers mainly male. There is a tendency to call reservations staff 'the girls' even by female managers who are younger than their staff. The role of the staff is usually perceived by the managers as low-level information processing, but we have already noted their profit-inducing potential.

We also have to ask what incentive there is for reservations staff to transform their role. Traditionally, at work, incentives are provided with money. People are paid for the increased risk their decisions involve. There is little evidence of performance-related pay in the hospitality sector. A crude incentive based on doubling wages for a day with no empty rooms would appear to be extremely radical, but would still lead to a significant increase in profit. As the impact of the informated worker becomes more apparent we shall see a new emphasis on remuneration as an incentive.

This remuneration is likely to be team-based, as, although decisions would be voiced individually, they would actually be based on the discussion and experimentation of the team. For maximum effectiveness information is shared and decisions become the province of all operatives. The information system itself could also be used in the calculation of the performance-related pay, which if it were calculated manually would be a convoluted and time-consuming process.

It is noticeable from other industries such as banking and insurance that one group that benefits significantly from information technology is women. IT appears to re-emphasize social skills like team-working and customer interaction. There is a shift towards a new type of employee: articulate, IT-literate, flexible, problem-solving and team-working. One result of this has been to help further to reduce the gap between average male incomes compared with average female incomes in those industries where IT has been a significant force.

Pay and information technology is an interesting issue for the hospitality industry. We have already noted how new systems bring in increasing responsibility, skill and control for the operatives, while reducing the amount of supervision. It does not seem that unreasonable to expect pay to go up in line with these changes. Daniel (1987) noted that one in five office workers see their pay go up in these circumstances, with the rest experiencing no change in their pay. The office workers that he surveyed had not observed as much change in the nature of their work as the hospitality operatives.

In the hospitality industry only one in ten operatives see their pay increasing as a result of the introduction of new information systems, and that is probably over-emphasizing the increase. One restaurant manager claimed that his hand-held devices for order-taking had reduced the number of waiters that were employed.

Consequently fewer waiters divided up the same amount of tips. In the view of the manager, pay had been increased as a result of the new computerized system. In the hospitality industry there is a particular failure to match changes in job skills and responsibilities with changes in remuneration.

This inability to tailor remuneration to changes in work practices is the hallmark of an industry resistant to change. Daniel's example was the (then) nationalized industries, but he noted how the hotel and catering sector was an even poorer innovator than the nationalized industries.

Another area where information technology impacts on staff is that of stress at work. Stress is sometimes associated with the work of high-level executives taking important business decisions rather than manual work. However this is a 'spurious assumption' (Blackwell, 1992, p.14). Stress is associated more with a feeling of a lack of control over the labour process and is therefore a feature of lower operative levels as well as being an expensive feature of our industry, not just in absenteeism, but in dysfunctional behaviour at work: alcoholism, personal disputes, inability to perform effectively (for example).

'The continuing development and application of information technology in the hospitality industry, would lead us to expect that stress amongst office and reception staff, in particular, would increase' (Blackwell, 1992, p.18). But we have already noted how, overall, new computer systems increase control over the way in which you perform your job, so contrary to these expectations, information technology is a reliever of work-based stress.

AUTOMATION

Outlined above is the side of information technology which, through the nature of the technology itself, rather than design, is transforming the hospitality industry. However, the 'automating' capability of IT is what concentrates the minds of hospitality managers. This is the use of computers as an extension of the Industrial Revolution: the 'smart' machine is used to reduce the number of staff by substituting humans with machines, and the tasks themselves are simplified. It also involves using the computers to monitor, measure and control the workforce, while giving staff little decision-making discretion.

There are numerous applications of this vision of information technology. Computerized key systems record and control the allocation of keys to staff which can reduce the need for administration staff. A 'clocking-in' system can be linked to a payroll system so that timekeeping is reflected in pay. Remote order pads for waiters can be introduced so that waiters can spend more time with customers as opposed to all that expensive 'interfacing' with food preparation staff. Computerized point of sales devices can measure the productivity of operatives: if they don't process enough customers there is the prospect of some form of disciplinary action. The increasing reliance on computerized in-room drink dispensers (Robobars) can reduce the need for floor staff to service hotel guests. Security cameras can reduce the need for security staff.

To an extent this is a positive force. Anyone who can compare calculating wages manually with using a computer system is aware of the advantages. Manual hotel reservation systems for large hotels were complex dinosaurs, which could make anyone aware of the benefits of automation. The problem with these types of applications is when the automating side is overemphasized and the informating side ignored.

In the assessment of their managers, most operatives were subject to less supervision, but one in four were actually subject to more. This is in marked contrast to Daniel's (1987) office workers, where most operatives did not experience any change in supervision.

In a study of a 900-room London hotel which was part of a large chain (Reeve, 1994, p.23) a member of reservations staff commented that she felt part of 'a conveyor belt system, just another passing number, not important'.

There is a significant minority of hospitality operatives using computers who experience work as mindless drudgery. Examples include operatives who have to transfer information from one system to the next, because the systems are not properly configured to exchange information directly. One operative in the above study was asked what she would say to her computer if it were human. Her response was: 'Can we do something else today?' In these situations people go to great lengths to personalize their environment, especially the cuddly toy stuck on the top of the computer.

TECHNOLOGICAL UNEMPLOYMENT

A good illustration of the tension between the automating and informating side of information technology is the question of technological unemployment. It is a relatively common belief that the introduction of technology has a substantial impact on the level of unemployment: more machines mean more unemployed. This argument suggests that information technology is responsible for decreasing staffing levels. Large numbers of hospitality managers believe that the main role of information technology is to reduce their workforce. Large numbers of trade unionists believe that information technology is a major reason for long-term unemployment.

There is no evidence that information technology has a significant effect on employment levels. The banking sector is usually quoted as an example of large-scale job losses at a time of a massive investment in information technology, yet here the job losses also coincided with an economic downturn which should take the real credit. Daniel (1987) noted that British offices that used computers were twice as likely to have taken on clerical, supervisory, technical, professional and management grades as those offices which were non-computer users. Hospitality managers who have successfully introduced new technology are aware that it rarely leads to job cuts. Sometimes the work is restructured and sometimes the number of tasks is increased, but it is exceptionally rare for redundancies to be caused by computers. If it is decided to cut the workforce, then this is normally accomplished by 'natural wastage': by not replacing leavers.

If you divide the number of bedrooms in a hotel by the number of employees, you get a figure for how labour-intensive a hotel is. The average computerized hotel has just over two rooms for each member of staff. The average non-computerized hotel has just under four bedrooms for each member of staff. Computerized hotels appear much more labour-intensive than small ones. It's true that larger hotels (which also tend to be more computerized) tend to be more labour-intensive anyway, but it is still impossible to argue that computerization causes job losses.

It is the strength of this 'computerized job losses' myth which demonstrates the strength of the *automating* vision of information technology. A large number of managers want computers to replace operatives. The extent to which it is *not* happening demonstrates the weakness of the *automating* capability of IT, when compared to the *informating* capability.

CONCLUSION

Hospitality operatives are increasingly finding that new systems give them more skill, interest, responsibility and control over how they perform their jobs. At the same time, in the opinion of their managers, they are needing less supervision. This represents a highly significant trend. Taken to its extreme, one possible long-term consequence is that management becomes superfluous. While I do not believe this is likely, it does raise long-term questions about the role of the manager in the computerized hospitality business. At the moment the number of managers are increasing substantially, and between 1981 and 1993 the annual rise in employment for managers and administrators was 2.8 per cent (Skills and Enterprise Network, 1995). What are all these managers to do?

Rather than the current state of play, where managers can suggest that 'staff were not an issue', it seems increasingly that the operatives will be able to say 'management was not an issue'. As Zuboff (1988, p.414) notes: 'Using the technology to its full potential means using the man to his full potential.'

DISCUSSION TOPICS

How might a managerless hotel or restaurant be organized? Advanced technological assistance can be used.

The term 'the girls' carries no pejorative connotations. Discuss to what extent stereotypes of sexual roles play a part in the hospitality industry.

To what extent do hospitality operatives resist responsibility in the workplace?

What is the role of supervision in motivating a workforce? Compare the ideal with experience.

To what extent do hospitality enterprises use placement students as their 'ideal' operatives?

4

Strategy: The Rational and Irrational in Business

Business strategy involves applying the rational to business behaviour: operational decisions are taken on the basis of envisaged goals or targets. We have already seen a potential for radical change in the chapters dealing with technology and consumers. Strategy is the attempt to meet these changing demands. 'Whereas in the past the emphasis has been on increased efficiency and cost reduction, today many other factors have emerged' (Bailey, 1993, p.150). Greater demands have been placed on customer service, quality, choice and flexibility as well as cost reduction. How the hospitality organization uses information technology to respond to this challenge is the subject of this chapter.

The first point to make about hospitality business strategy is its rarity. To a large extent management revolves around solving the day-to-day problems which are thrown up in running a business. This approach, usually characterized as 'fire-fighting', can take over the time and energy of all levels of management. If judgements about people are largely based on their ability to solve problems, it takes time, energy and courage to think systematically about reshaping the business, especially in cultures that do not favour risk-taking. Even in small, high technology firms in the electronics industry, Rothwell (1977) noted how their business policy grew organically from their problem-solving. This can be even more so for the hospitality industry.

The adoption of a written, company-wide corporate strategy or business plan is not the same as a strategy which reflects current business practice within all parts of the organization. The business plan may be provided for external consumption, e.g. the bank. It may have been written too far in the past and not reflect recent changes in the priorities or power structure of the company.

When a selection of over 200 randomly selected hospitality managers were asked if their organization had a business plan, only two-thirds said 'yes'. When those two-thirds were asked if it included any mention of information technology, a third said 'yes', a third 'no', but the remaining third did not know. The idea of the business strategy as an all-embracing corporate philosophy motivating all members of the organization is questionable.

What are the aims of people in business? First, it should be recognized that the main aim of employees is to earn the money to pay for the things they really want to do, or need: 'instrumentalized privation'. This can be proved by asking people to work for nothing. There are a number of subsidiary aims connected with the money, such as job security and a desire to increase remuneration levels, usually by promotion.

Owners of a business (either institutions or individuals) aim to increase their income levels by increasing profit levels. To achieve this aim they have various sanctions, traditionally connected with job security, to ensure that their employees work towards it. Business strategy is usually (see Chapter 7) a plan for the maximization of profits. Questions of growth, service quality and customer choice are important only in so far as they relate to the question of maximizing profits. Customer service is important not because it is important to be nice to people (though it might be), but because that way profitable repeat business will be generated.

It has to be said that business success is not always a rational process. If there was a statistical formula that guaranteed business success, business schools would have a very restricted curriculum. Success is the product of chance, location, the timely juxtaposition of a new service with a new demand. Success can catch the entrepreneur by surprise, after all the term does mean risk-taker: profit or loss, one minute advertising American Express cards, the next bankruptcy.

THE INFORMATION 'LOOP'

Information as lifeblood is an overused analogy, but it is a useful approach. The information flows from one part of the system to the next, carrying with it the preconditions necessary for any strategy. So what part does information technology play in this process of strategy building? Information forms the building blocks of the strategy. Without information, strategy becomes guesswork. In a randomly selected sample, taken in 1994, of just under 500 hospitality establishments, six out of ten were using some form of information technology. However, there was a big divide when it comes to size. If you use a definition of size based on the managers' own conceptions (Peacock, 1993a) the dividing line between small and large was 30 employees for restaurants and 80 for hotels. Using this line 95 per cent of large businesses were using some form of computers, but only just under half of small businesses had invested in this way.

At their simplest computers can be used to merely replicate an existing paper system. This is an inefficient use of the technology. Only when it is used to its maximum extent does it become part of the strategy of an organization. Gamble (1984) listed this spectrum of levels of computer use as clerical–administrative–tactical–strategic.

Most IT applications have a clerical and potential strategic importance. To see the potential strategic importance of information it is necessary to examine the variety of applications available to the industry. Basically these applications can be divided into those which are cost-centred and those which are revenue-centred. Starting with the cost side, the starting unit is the raw ingredient.

COST-CENTRED APPLICATIONS

Inventory

The measurement and control of the raw ingredient, from the sack of flour to the bottle of alcohol, has become one of the main applications of information technology. First, and most easily, the calculation of stock value can be accomplished very easily. A simple spreadsheet can calculate a revised stock value as you enter in new quantities.

Stock-taking as a major consumer of management time has decreased in importance. Hand-held computers can store the quantities as the manager moves around the stockroom. If the stock is equipped with printed bar codes (as is increasingly the case) then the bar code can be read with an electronic wand and the quantity simply typed next to the product description: a very fast process. As stock-taking becomes less onerous, its information can be more fully used. It is not unusual for a large hotel to buy all its season's banqueting alcohol in one batch. This is usually justified in terms of bulk discount, but it is not unreasonable to suggest that convenience plays a part. This stock value can then languish in cellars for a considerable period of time. Crown (a food and beverage control system vendor) note that the average public house holds over 20 days 'wet stock' when ten days is more than sufficient. Stock that is not being used (or 'turned around') is the equivalent of tipping cash down the waste disposal unit, as money is tied up in stock, thereby reducing cash flow and very possibly increasing the borrowing commitment of the business.

With a computerized inventory, purchasing can be based on demand and stock levels. In manufacturing industries this is part of what is referred to as 'just in time' purchasing. The computer has a record of your stock and a record of your desired reorder level and can print out a suggested order at the press of a button. This does not just reduce the amount of capital tied up in unused stock, but also reduces storage costs.

The Ingredient Database

Managing your ingredient database (computerized list) can become an art. Descriptive qualifiers are added after the name so that the computer can more logically order the ingredients. So 'diced chuck steak' becomes 'beef chuck diced'. In this way all the beef ingredients are listed together, and undiced chuck would appear next to diced chuck. Eggs could be broken down first according to type e.g. 'free range' or 'barn', then according to their numbered size.

Purchasing quantities are also stored for each ingredient. Eggs, for example, are rarely purchased individually but by the case; the purchasing unit would be one case. The stock-taker would then count the number of cases rather than the individual eggs. Sometimes though, different purchasing units would be entered for the same ingredient as there can be a variety of package sizes.

It is also necessary to have a new entry for each ingredient that comes from a different supplier. Prices, as well as purchasing quantities, can vary for an ingredient from each supplier. By listing the entries separately comparisons can be made.

It is easy to see how the ingredient database can become a total mess. An ingredient could be entered in a number of different ways. With different people entering data, the system could become unwieldy and unmanageable, resulting in a stock list double the length it should be. I have always found that the organization of the ingredients list is a good measure of how well the system is being used. However, perfection probably means it is not being used at all.

One of the main costs involved in storage is 'slippage', or, put more realistically, pilfering. While it is true that some types of ingredients can evaporate over time, the most common version of evaporation is being walked out of the back door. To some extent pilfering is a tolerated feature of the industry, but an inventory control system can at least measure what is occurring and, if required, control it. A regular and impartial stock-take is still needed to ensure that the system works.

Recipes

Recipes are constructed from the ingredients database, or sometimes from other recipes. The receipt database also needs a series of translating functions because the purchasing units will be different from the recipe units. Eggs may be bought by the case but they tend to be used individually in recipes. The situation is even more complicated if the purchasing units are metric (which they usually are) and units used in the kitchen are imperial. Even alcoholic beverages could have a recipe database, for example where cocktails are sold.

The purpose of the recipe database is to cost out the recipe. If the proportional difference between the selling price and the cost price is inadequate (the gross profit, or kitchen percentage) then the recipe is unlikely to be used.

The recipe database is one of the most under-used facilities of a food and beverage control system and there are a number of reasons for this. First, there is a considerable effort and expense involved in transcribing all of an establishment's recipes on to a computer. Recipe databases tend to be used where the recipes are standard across a chain of establishments, for example in branches of TGI Friday. Sometimes the ingredients database bears a remarkable similarity to the recipe database, as there is considerable use of convenience food or meals, for example pre-cut steaks or cut and frozen chips.

If the individual establishment prides itself on its unique creativity and changes the menu regularly, it is unlikely that the effort involved in updating the recipe database would be considered worth while. However the extensive collection of recipes which can make up a chef's repertoire, could be stored and accessed to advantage on a computer. Cross-referencing, printing, and costing can be handled much easier on a computer than with the old exercise books that you sometimes find in use.

In a heavily standardized chain of restaurants the recipe database could include instructions for the production of the dish and the garnishes that should be adopted. Sometimes there is a picture of the dish and how it is supposed to look, and it may be possible to store this picture on the computer. More usually today the information is stored in a book (with 'wipe-clean' pages).

Purchases

The combination of the recipe database, stock records and predictions on demand levels can be used automatically to generate orders. It is even possible that after a check these could be posted to the supplying company automatically by electronic mail (or fax card). It is also possible for the computer to use price comparisons from different suppliers in the calculation of the orders.

In practice, using the computer to evaluate possible suppliers tends to be done more by large, centralized purchasers where large bulk discounts are involved. An individual establishment tends to have a relationship with a supplier based to some extent on non-monetary considerations, such as delivery times or willingness to replace sub-standard ingredients. Also the quantities involved will be too small to make it practical to split orders between different suppliers.

The purchases system will record the order and then change the status of the order to a delivery, changing also the prices or quantities where appropriate. It will then be used in the handling of the invoices and statements from the supplier. Approximately a third of a catering establishment's expenditure could be controlled by this process. It is quite common for chains to keep an ingredient database and a purchase system, but not relate the two, especially when one of the two parts (usually stock control) is not computerized. When a delivery comes in, only the totals of the invoice are noted: cost and VAT or other taxes. These totals are then used as a record of expenditure by the controllers, but the establishment is not relating individual purchases to its inventory system. The end result is a very partial picture of how that particular establishment is operating.

Human Resources

If raw materials are a large part of the costs of catering enterprises, then staff and their associated costs are by far the largest element of hospitality enterprises costs. The most common application of information technology in this area is the administration of wages and salaries. Sometimes this might be contracted-out to an outside company, but these days there are cheap software packages available that can perform the task on a microcomputer. These packages come with specialized stationery for wages slips and regularly updated software to reflect changes (i.e. the Budget). It is possible to get the program to print all the cheques, if that is how the employees are paid.

Also commonly used in the hospitality industry are computerized personnel record systems. Every employee's details, such as address, next of kin, sickness record, can be recorded and easily accessed. As a replacement for the filing cabinet it is much more effective. However, this system can be taken a step further. Records can be analysed to look at labour turnover, absenteeism, timekeeping etc. Comparisons can be made, conclusions drawn and action taken. With the previous paper system, energy was taken up with just updating the records. With this system it is possible to take a more proactive approach. (The influence of the EU demanding the holding of more information on employees should be noted here.)

Take the problem of staff turnover for example. Hospitality management is largely complacent about annual percentages that can reach three figures. This has cost implications not only in recruitment and training but in revenue. Woods and Macaulay (1989) quoted a study which found that sales levels in restaurants with a high labour turnover were, on average, a quarter lower than sales of more stable companies. Addressing this problem has to be one of the key features of any strategy.

Payroll modelling can be used to look at costs in a number of ways. First, budgets can be compared quickly to actual expenditure. Labour cost can be related to sales to show which areas generate the highest profits. This can be taken to an hourly breakdown so that staffing is directly related to levels of business.

An interesting application of computerized human resource management is exit interviews. When a member of staff leaves it is good (if not common) practice to interview them to find out why they are leaving. Interviews conducted by personnel managers tend to be constrained by the personal relationships (and the question of references) involved. 'While departing employees were close-mouthed when interviewed by company personnel, they were very open about their real reasons for leaving in anonymous sessions with the computer' (Woods and Macaulay, 1989, p.90). Answering questions on a computer tends to result in much more honest answers which give good scope for analysis and problem-solving.

Computerized personnel systems can also assist with the beginning of a period of work. Although this is rare in the hospitality industry, an applicant's details can be entered into the computer and some initial assessment made on suitability. If, for example, personnel records indicate that a particular age group has a much higher turnover rate then that could be drawn to the interviewer's attention. While computer selections have not replaced interviews (outside some industries in America), it is difficult to make the argument that the subjectivity of the interviewer is any more effective than a statistics-based computer selection in making a correct decision. Some form of computer-based psychological profiling, analysis of previous staff records and a face-to-face interview would appear to be the most sophisticated staff selection process.

A computerized personnel system can also monitor the equal opportunities policies of a hospitality company, if it has one. Disadvantaged groups can be tagged in the system and their career paths or turnover records measured. In this way problems can be indicated and corrective measures taken. It has to be said that this is virtually unheard of in the British hospitality industry.

A final application of information technology to human resource management is training. Here IT has a number of possible applications at various levels. In the USA, the American Motel and Hotel Association developed a touch screen laser disc system to train new operatives in various tasks, such as making up a bed. The computer would be sited in its own room, and would be available at any time. The trainee would operate the program at his or her own pace and there would be a record of their progress. Here technology is used to provide a flexible and effective training solution; the user could even choose the language that they worked in.

This application was a little ahead of its time and the costs involved were too great to make the package widely available. However costs are falling and computer-assisted training will be an increasingly common aspect of a hospitality operative's work. At management level there is increasing use of computer-assisted simulations which enable the trainee to use 'play' to grasp the fundamentals of their work.

Training is not always seen as a part of a hospitality organization's strategy, but it is only through increased emphasis on training and education that employees can understand and implement corporate goals such as customer care or service quality.

Staff, purchases, recipes and inventory represent the cost side of the hospitality business. In a 'product'-centred business there can be a considerable emphasis on this side. The chef who sees his or her primary focus as the production of a dish of sufficient quality, rather than the satisfaction of a customer with this dish, is just one example. However, it is only one part of the equation. We now turn to revenue as an important element in this equation.

REVENUE-CENTRED APPLICATIONS

Reservations and Front-of-house

Reservations and front-of-house systems are sometimes marketed separately because they tend to be physically separate. Yet in most hotels they are part of the same system, whether paper or computer. A potential guest makes an enquiry which is answered by reservations, availability is checked, a price is agreed and the room provisionally booked. At some stage the room booking is confirmed and the change is reflected on the computer.

Yield management

Yield management is the maximizing of revenue through the manipulation of price points, and hence demand. It is a process that anyone goes through as they set a price and try to balance price and volume of sales: too high you sell nothing, too low and revenue may not cover your costs. Market haggling could be considered a form of yield management.

Computerized hotel yield management systems, once highly fashionable, have come under some criticism recently (e.g. Kimes, 1994). First, they are less appropriate in times of low demand. Second, if badly handled, they can lead to an increase in hotel customer dissatisfaction as they are transferred to another hotel. Third, it is questionable how much price differential for the same service people will accept as being fair. Variable pricing is largely accepted in air and rail travel and university tuition fees, but less so for hotel rooms. A hotel is unlikely to display a poster advertising its different rates for the same hotel room in the way that British Rail advertises its different price points.

A hotel system works by assessing the likely level of demand at each price point for a given day. It uses past records of sales to do this. Each type of customer and each point before the chosen day has its own pattern of demand. Basically the better off the customer (or customer's company) and the nearer the selling date, the higher the rate you expect.

A sophisticated system might 'close down' or stop the early allocation of rooms to a heavily discounted customer on the basis that last minute business, which expects to be charged a high rate, will arrive at the front desk. With the same level of business, a hotel using yield management can increase its room revenue by between 5 and 8 per cent (Boyce, 1991), when compared with a hotel not using a computerized yield management system.

Levels of demand for rooms fluctuate according to factors that the computer cannot envisage, e.g. rail strikes. Consequently its recommendations need to be monitored carefully. However, the greater its stored sales history, the more sophisticated and successful its predictions are.

Restaurants attempt to increase revenues by offering discounted meals during slack periods, but their potential for yield management is limited. Once a hotel has covered its costs the sale of an extra room is basically profit. There are marginal costs associated with the extra room sale, like stolen bath robes and cleaning, but these are negligible compared with the possible revenue. This gives hotels considerable flexibility when juggling prices.

Once the guest has arrived, check-in should be as simple as possible, ideally with the aid of a pre-printed form. Check-out involves the agreeing of the bill, with ideally all elements appearing in detail on one slip. This bill should include telephones, guest laundry, in-house restaurant or bar, room mini-bar and any other services that the client might have received.

This system should also have the facility to integrate with the housekeeping function so that the availability of cleaned rooms is constantly monitored and new guests can be directed to their rooms as soon as cleaning has been finished. Modern systems might have a facility for the housekeeping supervisor or room attendant to use a room's phone to dial a special code, indicating to the computer system that the room is ready to be allocated.

At this stage the reservation and front-of-house system, part of the property management system, is simply a clerical system which replicates the paperwork system which may have pre-dated it. The strategic implication comes with its subsequent use, either in a yield management role, through the analysis of its sales records, or through its links with other systems.

Modern hotel reservation systems are linked into a variety of external systems. The most famous of these are the airline-sponsored services such as Sabre and Sahara, which in their own jargon give 'worldwide electronic representation' to a hotel. Our American tourist can reserve a room in his London hotel at the same time as he buys his airline ticket. With one phone call he can purchase flight, hotel room and even car hire.

This method of reservation is becoming increasingly significant and will be covered more fully in Chapter 6. However, as homes and offices get increasingly incorporated into this computerized comunication network, more and more services will be purchased this way. At the moment, it is possible to have a menu faxed through to you. Within a decade it will be possible to look up the details of a restaurant, check availability and book a table all without leaving your own home. Unfortunately, when you get to the restaurant you may still have to wait an hour in the bar while they clear your table.

Point of Sale

Modern electronic cash registers are practically microcomputers in their own right, complete with their own range of microprocessors and sophisticated features. They might have the facility to act as time clocks for each server, the ability to deal with other currencies or a whole range of reports that can be produced on the till roll. The most common application of information technology in restaurants is point of sales systems.

Usually, an electronic cash register is considered to be part of an 'electronic point of sales' system when it is linked to a microcomputer or a wider computer-based system. Ideally the codes it uses are based upon the recipe database, which it uses in the form of 'price look-up' codes. Sales information is taken from the terminal and can be transferred into accountancy packages or into the property management system.

The modern tendency is to use technology to maximize the speed of service. Remote order pads may be used to take the order at the table, with the checked order being printed out in the kitchen. This means that the foodserver does not have to go into the kitchen to transfer the order. It also gets around the traditional problem of foodservers' handwriting. The itemized bill is printed out in detail on the restaurant printer at the completion of the meal. Sometimes the system can use customers' magnetic strip cards to take and record payment on the system. Even these card swipes can be portable, so that the waiter does not have to move from the table.

A crucial question is one of image. Sometimes the establishment can use technology to enhance its modern image, such as the Fifth Floor brasserie at Harvey Nichols, a restaurant on the top floor of a prestige department store in London's Knightsbridge. At other times a more traditional restaurant might want to hide the technology behind the duck press, which is a usually silver-plated, pre-Industrial Revolution artefact for squeezing the blood and juices out of duck. Both will use information technology to provide detailed sales records, fully itemized billing, efficient service and control of the sales process.

Marketing

A medium- to large-sized hotel will have people specializing in the sales and marketing function. It is their job actively to go out and promote the sales of rooms and they tend to deal more with group buyers such as travel agencies or large corporations. Their activities have to be co-ordinated with the reservations system in order to maximize revenue. A large, discounted, block booking organized by sales could be a serious handicap to maximizing revenue if room demand is buoyant. Often these types of considerations can lead to tensions within the hotel, and the use of a fully integrated property management system integrating sales and reservations is a positive force.

Frequently within a large hotel, the sales function runs marketing when ideally it should be the other way around. The Savoy Group and IBM have developed a computerized marketing system called 'Iolanthe'. This takes information from the reservations system and combines it with information extracted by the person taking the customer to the room. 'How was your journey, sir?' has been replaced with 'How did you hear about us?' or 'What particularly attracted you to this hotel?' An off-the-cuff remark from a guest about a new office opening nearby turned from a sales lead to sales of 400 room nights a year.

The marketing package can be used to carry out analysis. Customers can be analysed according to type of booking, market segment and reason for staying. This information can be broken down by country or even county, using the colour-coded maps that appear on the screen. If a particular American agent's bookings are up, this can be analysed and lessons drawn. The amount of time between the booking of a room and the client's arrival can be analysed and these 'lead times' can be used to tell sales when to target a particular group of clients, i.e. the point when they are considering booking.

Sales and marketing are brought together as an activity which, in hotels, is usually sales led. Sophisticated use of information strengthens the marketing activity which leads the sales team's activities and provides direction and focus. The marketing system has to be more than a supplier of a list of names, addresses and phone numbers of past customers for the sales team to start work on.

Particular hotel promotions can be correlated with bookings. Every promotion has a life cycle, so when the bookings created by an individual promotion start to tail off then a new promotion can be devised and launched. It is not just salespeople that benefit from improved information. Reservations now has the benefit of much better data and their role moves more into the sales role as they negotiate with potential clients.

Senior management benefit as they now have precise information, through their guest history, on the preferences of their clients. Properly used this can reshape the business as the hotel shifts from a product-centred to a customer-centred one. How attractive is that leisure complex? To what extent do customers want a fast check-in and check-out (where the receptionist's eyes never leave the computer screen), or a human/personal one (which takes longer)?

This type of strategic use of information technology can be adopted even before a hotel has opened. As we have already seen, Marriott conducted a large amount of consumer research, which they then ran through sophisticated statistical programs. The resulting information was then used in the development of their 'Courtyard by Marriott' concept (Crawford-Welch, 1993a). The traditional hospitality strategy is to produce a product and (to a large extent) simply let the market decide. What Marriott did was use the computer to let the consumer shape the product and service by calculating what the customer would be willing to spend extra money on. It is a use that can only increase.

Even in the context of a small restaurant the computer can have a significant effect on promotions. Knowing your sales mix can lead you to experiment with special discounts and promotions. A 'loss leader' (i.e. undercharging) on a fashionable premium lager may draw in the customers who will pay marginally increased prices on the less attention-gathering items. At the end of the promotion the marginal price increases remain. Having the information readily available enables the manager to use different techniques to maximize the revenue. If you want to check the extent of the overcharging on the more marginal items for yourself, use the price of a bottle of sparkling mineral water as a good example. In effect the computer enables the application of supermarket-style gimmicks or promotional devices to the restaurant sector.

Conference and Banqueting

One lucrative area for the hotel sector is conferences and banquets. Large block bookings of food and rooms are a significant source of income, especially for large hotels. The management of these functions can be fraught with difficulties, especially when you are not using a computer system. Traditionally a hotel will use a function diary, which in itself will create a lot of problems. In a large office, physically getting hold of the book can be a problem, let alone small practical problems like trying to write on top of a tippexed entry with a pencil.

A computerized system gives all operatives in this area access to the book. A customer rings up to make a change, their name is entered into the computer and their details are immediately available to be changed at will. This access is important because of the various stages involved before the conference or banquet. A tenuous request for information becomes a sales lead to be followed up, a booking turns into a discussion about the menu. Today, sophisticated systems can flag menu items that have been ordered for other functions which, if they are selected, reduces the workload for the kitchen staff.

Today's function sheets (a laborious task in a paper system) can be automatically generated by the computer. It becomes impossible to overbook, but instead a waiting list can be compiled. Reception and duty managers can find out what is happening where, by accessing their own terminal. Everyone is aware of the special needs of the customer, and even the length of time it takes to prepare a room can be programmed into the computer. The function's details are recorded to be used as next year's sales lead.

Financial information is readily available. For example, one problem for this department is the trade-off between food and beverage, and room revenue. If it is a heavy-drinking conference, then it is worth that additional discount on the room rate. Sometimes there is a tension between front office and conference and banqueting – both wanting to allocate the same rooms. The room split between the two departments can be organized on the basis of maximizing profits. Unsold rooms allocated to one section can be released to be sold to the other section.

Conference and banqueting involves handling a vast amount of small pieces of information. It's a job that is precisely suited to computerization. Information becomes more accessible, policy becomes more rational, time-consuming tasks are automated. The paper function book is still surprisingly common, but within ten years it will become a tool of the past.

Integration

Should all the different system applications be bought from the same supplier or should you 'pic 'n mix' from different suppliers? If you purchase from different suppliers then there is a problem of transferring information from one package to the next. This can be a major handicap. Too many hospitality operatives spend their time keying in the printout from one system on to the memory of another. Buying a 'total' multi-application package also tends to be cheaper.

On the other hand an integrated system rarely consists of the best possible modules for your establishment, nor does it tend to provide the flexibility and configurability that you may need. The best analogy is probably the purchase of a hi-fi. At the top end of the market it is rare to find systems with all components from the same supplier. At the bottom end it is more likely that the components will be of the same brand. There is no right answer, just a running debate. Ideally, software vendors could agree on some transfer protocols and make their modules more compatible with their rivals', but in reality they have a vested interest in tying purchases to their own range of products.

Each of the elements described above has both a mundane and superior aspect. The ingredients database could be a listing of stock, or the basis for a company-wide purchases system. The customer database could be a set of address labels for Christmas cards, or a tool for reshaping the product or service. Information technology has an enabling aspect, limited more by the skill, ambition and imagination of the system developer than the technical limitations of the hardware. One person's operations management assistance is the next person's strategic analysis. The previous examples have concentrated either on the revenue or cost side, however the more strategic applications come with the combination of both aspects.

COMBINED APPLICATIONS

Menu Engineering

Menu engineering is the combination of point of sales systems and recipe databases. There is a tendency to design menus on the basis of personal preferences, which are then modified on a trial and error basis. Because the quantity of information is so vast it is an exceptionally time-consuming and difficult process to work out on paper what is really happening with a menu. Menu compilers have a (superficial) impression of sales, but rarely is this balanced against the individual profitability of the dish.

A dish could be selling exceptionally well but a low profitability makes it suspect. Does it need re-pricing? Conversely, a highly profitable but poorly selling dish could be a potential goldmine which needs promoting or re-siting. Obviously a dish low in sales and profitability needs to be dumped quickly. The menu engineering application of a food and beverage control system can suggest a constant restructuring of a menu based on the preferences of the consumer. Even if the customer spend remained the same, then it is still possible to have a more profitable menu.

Promotion can be controlled in the same way that the pub chains are beginning to relate the increased sales of one selected product by one server to individual bonuses. Promotion becomes less a list of hints taped to a serving tray (Pizza Hut-style) and more productivity-related inducements.

In the same way that a properly set up property management system can produce predictions of levels of sales, a menu engineering package can use sales records to generate predictions which are the basis for management action. They could be improved upon, and every hospitality manager likes to think of him or herself as more accurate than the system, but as computerized sales records and sophistication grow, the more accurate computers become.

Accounting

Accounting has been talked of in terms of 'closing the loop' of information. Fundamentally, the key information to a profit-driven company is the movement of money. The applications listed above all involve the movement of money in some form and the accounting system acts as the consolidation of this information.

There is an irony in referring to accounting systems as 'closing the loop' in that they were often the first systems developed for hospitality organizations. Hotel accountants were introducing spreadsheets at the same time as the typewriter was being replaced by the word processor. Overall, the accounts function remains the most computerized function in the hospitality industry. Even in hotels, which tend to use a wider variety of IT applications than restaurants, it is the most widely computerized application, along with check-in.

Again, like the word processor, it was seen as an automator, with the flexibility and power of the spreadsheet perceived rather like an enhanced adding machine. At first there were few strategic implications in computerized accounts' systems other than the increased availability of financial information and the ease of its representation, e.g. graphs at a press of a button.

Gradually, however, that situation is changing. One of the beauties of an accountant's spreadsheet is the 'what if?' facility. By typing in revised figures the user can play with different scenarios and options, provided they remember not to re-save the spreadsheet at the end. 'At what point should we expand?' 'What would be the consequence of spending x money rather than y?' These type of questions can be easily explored with a computerised accounts system.

One all too common type of hospitality business which needs an obvious strategic re-think is the bankrupt or insolvent one. Basically, carrying on the way the company did before receivership is the recipe for a repeat disaster. One common option for the firm of accountants usually put in as an administrator is to computerize the work of the establishment. First, the prompt availability of information lets the administrators know how the business is operating, something which was usually not immediately available before the former owners ceased their managerial role. It is only through the availability of this financial information that change can be instituted and the profitability of the company turned around.

CONCLUSION

The picture painted above corresponds to an idealistic fantasy. Even among computerized restaurants less than half have a computerized food and beverage system. There is no hospitality enterprise in Britain that successfully incorporates all these elements of a successful application of information technology to strategic goals. Generally, industries other than hospitality have made a much better job of it: even in the related leisure or tourism industries. However, most hospitality companies have at least one of the applications listed above and this number is steadily increasing.

The ideal strategy links the elements listed above, not in a mechanistic, authoritarian way, but as a decision support system to an informed, imaginative, risk-taking group of decision-takers.

> *'What can we use the data for next?'*
>
> *(Paul Dermody of De Vere, quoted in HSSS Newsletter)*

Strategy needs information and it is through information technology that hospitality enterprises move beyond 'take it or leave it' responses to a more customer-focused approach to their business. To what extent they do, is addressed in subsequent chapters.

DISCUSSION TOPICS

What makes information technology significantly change the way in which a hospitality company takes strategic decisions?

To what extent do the hospitality managers you have come into contact with, take 'strategic' as opposed to 'firefighting' decisions?

What is the formula for business success?

What is strategy without information?

Discuss the suggestion that a Michelin-starred restaurant would never successfully utilize a recipe database?

What sort of person could best run a computerized hotel marketing system?

What could we use the information for next?

5

Managers: The Question of the Army Officer and the Piano Player

'Management' is one of those words which is associated with a particular point in time. The late twentieth century will be seen as the revolution in information technology, the end of the 'Cold War', the era of the hamburger and the triumph of the professional manager. In the same way that studying for a theology degree trained the clerics of (almost) bygone ages, business management degrees churn out the business administrators of the coming century. Management is accepted as one of those 'natural' functions necessary to the accomplishment of every task in developed economies.

It was not always so. For example, Britain's greatest era of construction and commerce was not marked by professional managers. If you needed a railway line built, the financiers and designers would employ independent gangs of men who were paid largely by results. These gangs were controlled by their leaders, who tended to be the more forceful, violent and skilled among them. They certainly were not socially distinct from their colleagues. It was these leaders who controlled the distribution of remuneration.

The professions of the time, from university lecturers to lawyers and bankers, were not characterized by managers, but tended to be self-governing, with administrative roles carrying no great authority, as they were subject to the consensus within the profession.

So what exactly is a manager? She or he has the authority to control (to a varying extent) the working life of the people working for the company or organization.

This involves the exercise of power or sanctions if the performance does not come up to expected criteria. Ultimately this power includes the possible dismissal of an employee. A specific manager may not have the ultimate power, but she or he will be in communication with a manager who does. The extent to which a manager can impinge on the operative's job security is the extent of the power of a manager.

There is also a 'clean' element to the concept of a manager. Trainee managers do not expect to work in dirty manual jobs or situations requiring great physical exertion, once they become managers. A suit is the uniform of the British manager: not a pair of dirty overalls. There is a social dimension to the concept, with the manager expecting a higher level of remuneration. Managers tend to have higher levels of education and their jobs are more sought after. On visits to hotels, I am sometimes struck by how the hospitality industry appears to be composed of managers managing operatives consisting almost entirely of assistant managers, management trainees, management students on placement and other management 'wannabees'.

This perception of a manager as an organizer of work is a relatively modern construct. It is large-scale office work which is traditionally associated with the rise of the professional manager. As the entrepreneur lost direct control over the clerks ranked outside his office, he needed people to exercise his authority for him. Ownership itself shifted from individuals to large organizations (such as pension funds) which needed direct authority to be exercised for them.

Associated with these structural changes was a shift in the way people perceived authority and its purpose. Politically, this is usually associated with the late nineteenth century rise of the Prussian state. The Prussian army was the product of Frederick the Great's childhood obsession with mechanical toys. The professionalism of its officer/management class, the emphasis on unquestioning obedience, combined with a stress on bureaucratic controls and regulations created a totally new force in world politics. This army swept all before it.

The existence of mass education can be said to owe more to the Prussian example than to anything else. Even our traditional British policeman's helmet is based on the Prussian soldier's. The British officer class, previously a drinking club for ex-public school boys, was forced, to some extent, to adapt.

It is this military model of management which has always figured prominently in the conception of British hospitality managers. Until relatively recently a proportion of the latter gained their first management experience in the military. The hospitality industry has been recognized by its workers as a highly autocratic industry. Instructions are given and expected to be followed. There is historically, little emphasis on discussion or any consensual style of management.

The hospitality industry has a fair claim to be the most authoritarian industry in Britain. A manager interviewed recently, fresh out of the Army Catering Corps, noted that 'you can't just order people about any more'. Ironically, he was finding the industry more autocratic than the army. Instructions and directives appear to form the mainstays of the hospitality industry.

To some extent this meets with the approval of operatives. If you have followed your instructions then the remaining work-time can be seen as your own. If you don't wish to engage your brain in your work, then an autocratic management style can be popular. There is evidence that the autocratic management style of the hospitality industry is no more unpopular than the more democratic management styles prevailing in other industries. However, it does seem that this autocratic style is less popular with younger employees and with women than with men.

The emphasis on instructions and silent, if not unthinking, obedience also complements a strongly bureaucratic tendency with its precise role definitions and exact rules for behaving. White (1973) has noted how a modern kitchen can still have over ten different levels of authority, and within hotels and restaurants jobs are characterized by strong differentiation. One food server can serve the food while another serves the alcohol. One hotel operative can hold the front door open, one conducts the check-in and a third carries the bags upstairs. Within the industry this strong demarcation is seen as natural and functional.

It is possible to view the large hotel kitchen as part of the Victorian autonomous work-gang tradition rather than part of twentieth-century managerialism. The *chef de cuisine* is more likely to identify himself (overwhelmingly) as a chef rather than a manager. Often his authority rests on the force of his personality and his craft skills, which he may only demonstrate rather than practice. Junior chefs come under the authority of the head chef rather than managers generally, and they have a strong sense of their distinct identity. It used to be a tradition that if hotel management arrived unannounced in a kitchen (in their morning suits), then junior chefs could pelt them with food. Sometimes when a good head chef leaves, he or she may take a number of the junior chefs on to the next establishment. While there is an attempt to make chefs 'kitchen hands' subject to general management, the survival of the well-paid, semi-autonomous head chef seems assured as long as hotels and restaurants are judged on the quality of their food.

However, outside the semi-autonomy of the kitchen brigades of large hotels, operatives are controlled by a relatively highly autocratic and bureaucratic breed of manager, characterized by a non-consensual style of decision-making. In an industry as large as the hospitality industry, there are always exceptions: both companies and individuals. It is worth commenting that even companies with a strong commitment to employee participation (such as Scott Marriott) have managers who find their company strongly centralized when compared with other industries.

One symbol of the degree of employee consultation is the position of trade unions. Even given the relative decline in the success of trade unions, the hospitality industry has always been marked by its anti-union policies. Trade unions have never achieved significant membership within the industry and a large part of that is due to the traditional hostility of hospitality managers.

Apart from the lack of employee consultation and highly differentiated job definitions, the hospitality industry is also characterized by a strongly segmented departmental culture. At its most extreme, this is the traditional hostility between the food service and food preparation departments. However, this is only the tip of the iceberg and it could be argued that it is so obvious because the two departments are forced to be in regular contact with each other. Other departments have their strong patterns of loyalty and identity formed almost in adversity. These departments are controlled by managers who see their departments as their own territory. Among hospitality managers this is characterized as 'empire building'.

The managers in these departments have a vested interest in minimizing their problems; a problem internal to a department reaches a new level when it becomes visible to those outside the department, reflecting unfavourably on the competence of the manager. To an extent, the visibility of the problem can become as much of a concern as the problem itself. One interviewed hotel manager defined success as 'making sure my general manager is not aware of any problems'.

The autocratic, regulated, segmented character of the hospitality industry is usually referred to as 'mechanistic'. Wood (1992, p.15) notes that 'mechanistic organizations are characterized by high levels of bureaucracy, extensive specialization and division of labour and hierarchical structures of control'. However, a feature of this type of organization is its inefficiency, and any member of the organization who wants to achieve things may decide to bypass the formal organization. In this way a parallel 'organic' structure develops, based on personal contacts and reciprocity (exchanges of favours). Even an organization as mechanistic as the army has a parallel organic structure (traditionally based on non-commissioned officers), working to its own agenda.

The relationship between the culture of the industry and information technology is a crucial one. Daniel (1987, p.273), in his survey of British industry's attitude to advanced technology commented on the link between management's attitude towards consultation and its attitude towards information technology. He found that contrary to popular perceptions 'management which did not recognize manual unions tended to be relatively passive, conservative and even apathetic'. It appeared that managers who consult with the workforce were not just more likely to use information technology more successfully, they were also more likely to introduce it in the first place.

The concept of 'corporate culture' has been attacked recently. When it is merely the stated philosophy of senior management, it can often be contrasted with their actions, and still more so with the actions and attitudes of their operatives. Here, the term of organizational 'culture' is used to express the thoughts and actions of all members of an organization. An organization has a 'structural repertoire' from which it chooses its course of action from a range of options. This repertoire is different for each organization: limited for an unimaginative one, extensive in the case of a creative organization.

The adoption and use of information technology in the hospitality industry is the product of this structural repertoire. The autocratic and bureaucratic tendencies within the industry have already been noted and these traits are reflected in the available choices.

CONTROL

The first desire of the autocratic hospitality manager is control. At the simplest this is the 1980s' habit of attempting to replace humans with machines. We have already noted how it rarely works, but it still figures prominently in the minds of hospitality managers. Point of sales systems become measures of individual performance and productivity. A McDonalds point of sales system can give details about the efficiency of its operatives. In the same way Sainsbury's system can detect the slower check-out person, low individual productivity can be detected: 'allow closer scrutiny of staff performance' (sales literature). Usually this information is used as a pressure on staff, perhaps in the form of league tables, rather than a direct attempt to remove the slower worker.

A telephone logging system can be justified on the strength of its ability to record unsanctioned use of the telephones by staff. Misuse of telephones by a multinational workforce can be a serious concern for management. The system can also be used by hotel security to track down defaulting guests. The numbers that the guest dialled can be called up and the identity of the missing guest detected. Again, the mere existence of this system can act as a deterrent.

Handling of cash becomes another major concern of hospitality managers. With the endemic high turnover of staff and the use of casual labour, some hospitality managers have doubts about the honesty of their cash handlers and a point of sales system can pinpoint the individual server where there are any shortfalls. This is not a foolproof solution, more a motivating factor for the purchase of these systems.

With a paper system, it is not uncommon for a food server to 'lose' the bill for the group of friends that he or she is serving. With a busy restaurant the paid bills are not always matched up with the food orders, so good friends are able to eat and drink for free. A point of sales system will be able automatically to match up the food and drink orders with the bills, and any discrepancies can be printed out with the food server's name.

An inventory system can be used to match sales with stock and again discrepancies (variance reports) can be flagged. The discrepancy could be a dropped bottle, or a burned joint of meat, but after a certain point (perhaps 5 per cent of sales) it becomes a cause for management action.

Inventory systems are more common with alcoholic beverages because their theft is more significant to the finances of the business. For an employee intent on pilfering, alcohol is more attractive than food because food tends to be bulkier than the same value of alcohol. Some food also has a tendency to drip, and besides, bottles of alcohol are easier to resell. Premium lagers, i.e. those that you drink from the bottle to indicate your purchasing power, tend to be a particular problem. A manager at the First Leisure Corporation, which runs a variety of leisure complexes, noted that half a percentage improvement in their alcohol gross profit would translate as an extra £1 million group profit.

The use of point of sales and food and beverages control systems can seriously restrict the possibilities for staff pilfering. It does not rule them out entirely. To steal, you have to bypass the system entirely, like the bar staff who buy their own alcohol, sell it in the bar and pocket the profit. They have to make sure they do not 'ring up' the sales on the point of sales device. Even this fiddle can be overcome with management vigilance, or even the use of video cameras (not entirely unknown).

The focus of the management and its efforts to control the workforce is primarily on the cost side of the business. Managers are principally assessed on their ability to control costs: reduce the number of staff, reduce purchases, cut back on slippage of stock. The revenue side is seen as something largely outside the control of the manager. Even something as esoteric as the situation in the Middle East can impact on hospitality managers, through terrorism fears affecting the number of tourists.

If the revenue side is seen as the product of a relatively fixed product mix, then it is difficult for hospitality managers to think that they have considerable influence in this area and the emphasis on the cost controlling side can override income considerations. It is possible that a slow hamburger server may be more than an inefficient cost unit, the server may be talking to the customers and generating goodwill and future business. It is possible that the individual establishment's promotion and presentation may be financially more significant than a dishonest barperson on the staff of that establishment. However, the primary focus of today's hospitality manager's use of information technology is that dishonest barperson.

In the words of the sales literature, product X 'spots the fiddles, management's greatest problem' (*sic*); product Y: 'If used on a regular basis, it can reveal virtually every type of sham, scam and impropriety a devious bartender can perpetrate against your business.'

One of the ironies of this type of approach is that managers can be the fiddlers themselves. Even if they are not stealing, they can be aware of the theft and tolerating it. After all 'waiters would not wait and chefs would not create unless they were similarly assured that part of their total income would come from fiddles' (Mars, 1982, p.18). Does the intelligent, informed manager want to double his staff turnover figures by clamping down on fiddling? After all, in the service sector, if the customer is happy it is irrelevant whether s/he has been fiddled.

Mars (1982) has an excellent account of a group of British hotel workers who overcharged for drinks to the tune of £10,000, over a period of months. The manager was aware of the overpricing but in his defence (at his trial) noted how it helped to keep up stocks and increase profits: pilfering was low, as it was the customer who was being ripped off, not the company. The manager also claimed that head office was well aware of the practice. This particular fiddle came to light after the manager removed an operative who was stealing stock *and* overcharging. She informed head office, who then could not pretend not to know what was happening. In situations like this, the food and beverage control system could probably be used as an aide to systematic fiddling.

Although management is based on power, a key element is the use of negotiation. The manager who phrases directives as 'can you do me a favour?' may not expect anyone to say 'actually, no', but there is still the recognition that there is a reciprocal level to the relationship between manager and operative. If the operative is asked to perform a series of unusually unpleasant jobs, then the operative might expect the manager to provide some recognition. In the hospitality industry this is unlikely to be a Christmas bonus. It is possible that recognition of services rendered may be tolerance to lateness the following day, permission to make a personal phone call, or a blind eye to a pilfered chicken. All three could be considered stealing; all three are common in the hospitality industry. The hotel manager in the example above could be seen as taking this reality to a logical conclusion: after all, he had happy customers, low turnover of staff and good profits. What more can a good hospitality manager provide?

'EMPIRES'

Information technology has significant implications for the traditionally rigid departmental structure of the hospitality industry. At the moment, the strong divisions impact on the use of computers, rather than the other way round. The food and beverage manager may have a computerized inventory system imposed on him or her, usually after losing out in a power struggle with the accounts manager. The food and beverages manager is automatically going to be defensive, any problems will become magnified and failures of the new system will become 'the computer's fault'.

Sometimes the strong demarcation lines can be eroded by technology. We have already noted how a strongly divided hospitality organization has little incentive to share information. This is inefficient: information needs to be shared in large hospitality organizations.

Front-of-house staff need booking details from reservations, housekeeping needs occupancy predictions from reservations, reservations needs to know what marketing is planning, sales have to liaise with front-of-house over bookings, food and beverages need details on the banquets that sales have booked, as well as expected occupancy levels from reservations and front-of-house. These exchanges in information are just a fraction of the information exchanges in an organization: the lifeblood of the organization. Failures lead directly to unsatisfied customers, loss of revenue, or overproduction: lower profits.

With a strongly departmentalized organization the flow of information is not an easy process. The hospitality industry has a tradition of face-to-face interaction of managers with regular meetings. A large hotel might have an early morning meeting of the management team, but is more likely to have a weekly one. The frequency and character of these meetings are the product of the personalities of the senior management. The meetings are rarely detailed enough to cope with all the information necessary for the co-ordination of departments and so are supplemented with written communications.

Traditionally, the non-verbal communication is accomplished with a flow of memos which is both slow and cumbersome. They need to be produced, sent, read, prioritized and then acted on – perhaps. Sometimes, part of this process is departmental managers using memos to protect themselves from other departments. In the quasi-military male jargon of hospitality managers this is known as 'covering your backside'. If you anticipate a problem, a memo is sent which flags the problem and indicates its source or solution as the province of another department or section of the hierarchy. Ideally the memo should not be read on receipt, but should subsequently be flourished when the problem has come to a head: 'but I warned you about this in my memo of . . . '.

This type of approach does not fit a sophisticated use of information technology. A fully-integrated, modern hotel has an open system where departmental information is readily available to those with access to a computer. This means that the problems that dominate the work of a departmental manager are visible to other managers. Information has become a shared resource and that has significant implications for the role of the manager.

This theory has been termed 'visibility theory' by Buchanan and McCalman (1988). In a study of the Glasgow Holiday Inn, Buchanan and McCalman mapped the dramatic changes brought about by information technology. In the 1960s and 1970s there was a relatively common belief that computers would replace middle and junior management. The authors wanted to show that information technology was enhancing the role of the manager and that there was no possibility that the role of the middle manager would be 'automated'.

In the study, it was found that the internal problems of a department could be disguised no longer. One senior manager was quoted as saying: 'We do not hide anything. All of our heads of department know exactly how our business is doing.' Management became a co-operative venture where the management team acted together to improve operational efficiency. The very term 'management team' took on a whole new significance. As Buchanan and McCalman noted: 'shared information, shared confidence, shared visibility and shared pressure encourage a cooperative approach to management decision-making, reducing opportunities for power struggles and interdepartment conflicts.'

The study was conducted ten years ago and there is no doubt that visibility theory forms part of the 'informating' capacity of information technology. But its case can be overstated: the Glasgow Holiday Inn (now Scott Marriott) was part of a chain with an exceptional commitment to information technology, establishment autonomy and employee empowerment.

In the industry as a whole the battle between the traditional autocratic culture of the hospitality manager and the informating capability of the new technology is far from over. The picture presented above is untypical for hotels, even those with the same level of computer usage.

A good illustration is the use of electronic mail, which was not common at the time of Buchanan and McCalman's study. With electronic mail (e-mail), notes can be typed directly into your machine and sent directly to another e-mail correspondent. It might be possible to look at the appointments diary of another manager, send a response back immediately to a memo, or send a memo to a variety of managers, all without getting up from your chair.

Although e-mail is increasingly common within the industry, it is rare to see it fully used. Its openness and accessibility clash with the inclinations of most hospitality managers. Anyone who has noted a department in a hotel carefully (and skilfully) configuring their e-mail system so that only intra- (rather than inter-) department communication is possible, would be forced to question the current force of visibility theory. A manager who perceives a new system as a source of control is unlikely to stress the communication side. It is only through using information technology to communicate that it takes on its full role.

Ultimately, communications through the computer take on all the characteristics of face-to-face contact, with the 'computer coffee break' where managers sit at the computer and use it to gossip with other managers. This way they can express their genuine work interests: how incompetent/stupid their bosses are, how nasty the company is and who is sleeping with who. These human social contacts are vital to the operation of a company: at the very least to let off steam and relieve stress. At their best these social contacts can become an 'unofficial' way of making contacts across the company and solving mutual problems.

This side of technology can be seen in the 'cybercafés' of inner cities, where the consumer can nibble a croissant, sip a cappuccino, and use the café computers to chat to a stranger in Australia, or make a date with someone they have never seen. The 'information super highway' is all around us. It will be ironic if hospitality managers continue to cut themselves off from it, while their customers are tapping into their modem-linked laptop computers immediately above them.

INFORMATION AS POWER

One medium-sized hotel studied recently had purchased a property management system which was effectively sabotaged by the reservations manager keeping key information off the system. He had built up considerable contacts and expertise with key clients of the hotels. The reservations staff could not make decisions without referring to him because he was holding key information. By putting his information on the computer (block bookings etc.) the reservations staff would have been able to work independently. However his skill and expertise had taken him a long time to acquire. It is true he felt unable to go on holiday, but if his information had been held in the system, he felt his position would be undermined. He would no longer be the indispensable person.

Information is intimately connected with power. If you define power as the 'authoritative allocation of resources' then what legitimizes and supports this authority is information. If a manager is accused of performing inadequately, any sanctions taken against that manager are usually supported with information. Control of information is control of people. In the hospitality industry salaries are generally closely guarded secrets, if all income details were released, uproar could result. Establishment profits are rarely expressed to operatives, partly through the fear that they may be used to support wage claims.

Traditionally, the role of the manager is enshrined in this control of information. A large part of the manager's work is the transfer of information through words, reports, memos. The manager selects what information is to be presented to whom, in the same way as the manager above. A 'need to know' policy can be part of the hospitality manager's code: there is no automatic right to information.

This perception of the role of the manager as information transferrer clashes with information technology. No longer does information lie in a huge disorganized pile on the manager's desk, with overflows stacked on the floor. This information is available on the system. The manager may configure the system to restrict access to information, through the use of access codes. Sometimes systems are sold on this basis: 'staff are only able to access functions permitted by the management'. But this is a process doomed to failure. As operatives realize that information that could enable them to better perform their jobs is available without going through the manager, they will bypass that manager. Codes and passwords will be exchanged.

Hospitality managers dislike the idea of open systems with easy access to information. And they would claim that some information must be hidden: personnel records for example. However, employees have a legal right to access their own personnel record stored on the computer. Sensitive company information can always be used by a manager moving to a rival, but information by its nature is constantly changing. In my research I have found that the secrecy of a company is directly proportional to its business confidence. A successful company is proud to show people around and publicize its achievements. An unsuccessful one will not co-operate, claiming the need for confidentiality. As a whole the hospitality industry is marked by relatively high levels of secrecy.

BUSINESS EFFICIENCY

Information must have a direct relationship with business efficiency. If computers do not generate more profits than their costs, they are superfluous. Their costs can be major undertakings for any hospitality establishment. A small restaurant might be able to set itself up with a system for under £2,000, but a large hotel could spend £500,000 on an integrated system. If using the system results in 50 fewer employees then the system might pay for itself within six months, but we have already noted that it is rare for information technology to reduce overall staffing levels.

The average productivity (sales for each employee) for hospitality establishments (*circa* £35,000 in Peacock's 1994b London study) is not significantly different for computerized and non-computerized establishments. Productivity is higher with computerized hotels, but this is caused by the size effect, that is, larger establishments generate higher productivity simply because of their size, and if you take this effect out, then computers do not have a statistically significant effect on productivity. Remanco's claim of a possible 6 per cent increase in profits after the installation of one of their systems could be seen as largely a combination of sales puff and wishful thinking.

These days, managers in large hotels would find it inconceivable to manage the establishment without the assistance of computers. However, it does appear that they are not generating significant improvements to the finances of the hotel. The £500,000 expenditure is a regular commitment rather than a one-off payment. Systems are upgraded, faster hardware bought, new departments computerized. The life of a system depends on the policies and personalities of the establishment, but an industry average is just over five years. Some establishments give their systems a life of just three years. Other managers have trouble with the concept of a restricted lifespan for IT systems. The end result is often a considerable expenditure for a negligible benefit.

In the hospitality industry there is no relationship between relative technological sophistication and business success. With other service industries, from banking to airlines, there is an undoubted correlation. However it would be wrong to suggest that 'state of the art' computerized hotels or restaurants automatically dominate their market sector.

Interviewer: 'Would you say you were using the system to its full capacity?'
Manager: 'We must be, otherwise it wouldn't keep on crashing.'

Rather than suggesting that information technology is a marginal issue, which is a common response for hospitality managers, the problem lies in the perspectives of the managers. The systems are not achieving what the managers expect as there is this huge gulf between expectations of hospitality managers and the real contribution that information systems can provide for business objectives. We have already noted the failure of information technology to reduce staffing levels and this is a common part of the manager's expectations. The manager who perceives a new system in terms of increased control could also be disappointed; sometimes the manager could end up with less control. In essence, information technology is going to provide improved information and this is difficult to quantify. A reduction in pilfering could be charted on a graph, but a menu restructuring brought about through improved information has cost benefits that could be hidden by market fluctuations. The mismatch between the culture of hospitality managers and the potential benefits of information technology is hindering its effectiveness.

In effect the hospitality manager treats information technology as an enhanced paper system. IT is fitted into existing work patterns and practices which are simply inappropriate in deriving the maximum benefit from the new management information systems. Possible restructuring and new ways of working that stress the informating side of the technology are largely ignored at the moment. Information technology is about ways of handling a constantly changing flow of information. Sometimes modern hospitality management appears to seek structure and rigidity almost as a response to this image of constant change.

To put it another way, one of the concerns for the hospitality manager is the organizational chart: it provides structure and a point of reference. At the moment information technology is being used to produce the charts in a more attractive manner: neat arrows and perhaps some shaded boxes. However this is a long way from Tapscott and Caston's (1993) programme for an effective IT strategy. Their point 5 was 'Chuck the Chart' as the only way to effective systems planning.

This reluctance to embrace change can be seen in the evaluation of new systems. Investment appraisal is a difficult area for the hospitality industry. Rarely is it quantified or even documented. If the ideas justifying the purchase of the system are not put down on paper, how can the decision be evaluated in the light of performance? Even appraisal methods as basic as 'payback periods' are rarely fully used to justify the expenditure. Sometimes this vagueness can work to IT's advantage. In my own institution if I were to ask for some esoteric and obscure piece of IT, I would stand a possibility of getting it, without people exposing their ignorance by asking me what it is. However, if I were to ask for six pencils, that would be automatically cut to two, on the grounds that it is an obvious over-order.

The 'Upgrade'

Justifying the expenditure is a difficult question with brand new systems, but considerably more complicated when an existing system is being replaced with a more 'up-to-date' one. Once a system is installed it develops a force and momentum of its own. Questions of speed and integration become paramount. The user of the system wants the latest 'much-improved' model.

It is not uncommon for an upgrade to be justified on the grounds of the improvements it will bring about compared to no system at all. However, the crucial question is the *extra* improvements it will bring about. The upgrade might cost more than the original system for only a marginal improvement. With technical specialists, the technical data (e.g. speed and reliability), can become their own driving force, leading logically to the next purchase. In fact, shortcomings are an inevitable feature of any system that is being fully used. If managers consider a system to be perfect, then they are not using it.

Sometimes the question of the functionality of a system is simply not addressed. The sales literature of 'solutions' firms can place a disproportionate emphasis on the technical specifications of their hardware, while the more important details of the functions of the system are minimized. Debate on a new purchase can concentrate too much on the relative number of features of competing packages and not enough on their suitability to a specific establishment's needs. Sometimes this can reflect the lack of confidence that the manager has in his or her own abilities.

'Specifying their information needs' will become the core skill of the hospitality manager, not so much deciding what they are going to do with their information, but deciding what information they are going to need for the effective performance of their roles. Information has a Plasticine quality and needs to be grabbed and moulded by the manager. In one large hotel which acquired a control system for alcoholic beverages, the managers spent weeks reorganizing their cellars to match the stock order on the computer. A more effective solution might have been to reconfigure their stock lists on the computer: a relatively simple hour-long task.

It is the more unsophisticated systems, where the manager can manipulate and configure the data, that are an unexpected success in the hospitality industry. In my research, the software package most commonly mentioned by hospitality managers is Lotus 123. Lotus is a general type of spreadsheet package where the manager has to set up the information from scratch. It is as common as the most widely-used package of specifically hospitality software (Innsite). A hotel can spend £300,000 on hospitality systems, but if you ask a numerical question then the answer could easily appear on a £200 spreadsheet.

Spreadsheets were the application which made the microcomputer popular with managers. It is through the use of spreadsheets that the manager can 'play' with data: manipulate, experiment, make mistakes, maybe come up with strokes of genius. It is the 'informating' side of information technology applied to the manager.

The 'hybrid manager' is a type of manager who combines skills in information technology with general management skills. It marks the direction of the future. One day hospitality managers will be able to interact with their computer-aided design packages to construct the environment that they are striving for. They will be able to 'wander around' their computer-simulated restaurants as if they were inside the computer and be able to see how it feels for the customer or member of staff. In the same way the modern manager needs to interact directly with the information presently available: to make sense of it, work out what is wrong, decide on changes, envisage how these changes will be implemented, and communicate these thoughts to others. This sea change will be a slow process for the hospitality industry.

DISCUSSION TOPICS

To what extent do different departmental roles within a hotel correspond to different personality types?

'A slug on the pavement or a road warrior on the information super highway.' Which category does the modern hospitality manager fall into?

Is computerized social contact between hospitality managers, unrelated to work, a waste of company time and money?

How do you justify the purchase of an oven, and how might you justify the purchase of a point of sales system?

6

Corporations: Discipline in the Corporate Machine

When you talk to managers from the head office of a large hospitality company, they often refer to themselves using the analogy of the human body. The head office is the 'nerve centre' or the 'brain' of the operation. The term 'head office' carries its own body analogy. Without the brain/head office the body would supposedly be a lifeless mass, characterized by the odd twitch. It is a vision of the company which is rarely shared by managers within the establishments themselves. They see themselves as the productive end of the company and privately they may question the positive contribution of head office to the service-selling business. It is a tension which is endemic to a large hospitality corporation.

For a contract catering company like Gardner Merchant the fear is even more tangible. If the local manager develops a good relationship with the client, i.e. the person responsible for buying in the catering for their own company, then it is possible for the local manager to suggest that the catering becomes independent. The management fee that was paid to head office could then be divided between the client and the local (now independent) manager. This is not as uncommon a situation as contract catering companies would have us believe. It is not just a question of whether the local unit would perform better without the centre, it is whether the contribution of the centre more than compensates for the cost of it? Do we need centralized control, and if we do, how is it to be exercised? These are real questions for both sides of large hospitality companies.

We have already seen how information technology is sold to hospitality managers as an instrument of control: before computerization the manager is 'virtually relegated to the passive role of observer', but 'the technology now exists to change all that' (systems sales literature). In the same way, information systems are sold to head offices as a way of overseeing their outlets: product X 'is a food and beverage package that allows fully distributed operation, providing head office control over multiple branded outlets' (sales literature).

For the hospitality industry as a whole, if the establishment is a member of a chain then the manager is much more likely to be using a computer system. Multiples are twice as likely to be computerized as non-multiples; independent establishments are four times as likely to be uncomputerized. A high proportion of hospitality systems are imposed on establishments. When establishment managers who worked in a chain were asked who originated the idea for the system they were using, four out of ten did not know. This tends to suggest that it was not an establishment manager who had come up with the idea for a new system. Of the remainder almost five out of ten answered that the idea came from head office.

These managers are using information technology simply because they have been told to. Not only do they not choose the system, but the managers have a limited say in how the system is to be operated. The system reflects the priorities of head office, and those are not necessarily the same as the priorities of the individual establishment.

Head office will perceive a number of significant advantages to centralized purchasing of management information systems. First, their corporate buying power should be able to negotiate a better price, and once the system has been installed they are in a better position to pressure for improved support or training. Second, the provision of head office specialists should mean a better selection of system. For a large company, expenditure could run into tens of millions of pounds and head office needs to control this centrally.

A third consideration is that the centre wants to ensure that it is possible to transfer data between its various establishments and the centre. Ironically, centralized purchasing is very unlikely to produce standardized systems in all of its outlets. There is always a historical legacy: priorities and systems are changed and it takes time and money for all outlets to catch up. Hilton International, for example, is currently using three property management systems: Fidelio, HIS and their own version of Champs.

Technological Inertia

If you have spent millions of pounds on hardware for your corporation, then it is very difficult to keep up with improvements in computers. Those purchases, known as 'legacy systems', fix the company at a point in time, and it is difficult to justify the upgrade.

At the moment, the hospitality industry is very slowly upgrading to 'Windows'-compatible PCs. This is a slow process, because so many of the existing computers are not capable of running the current version of Windows. Information technology is a constantly tilting playing field.

The question of the compatibility of the hardware and the software is crucial. There are degrees of compatibility: complete incompatibility means typing in the figures from one system into another. Sometimes though, the data has to go through a translation procedure and this can take time. Ideally the centre wants to have daily performance figures by the end of the day and to be demanding explanations by the following day.

Essentially the centre feels that if information is channelled through itself, then there are a number of advantages for the company worldwide. There are an increasing variety of ways in which information can be collected at the centre and then distributed to the individual establishments.

INFORMATION GATEWAYS

Let us now turn to how that information is centralized and controlled by head office. First, the centre can ensure the conformity of the interfaces to central reservations systems. Travel agents using systems like SABRE, AMADEUS, APOLLO or GALILEO can ensure that they have access to hotels in a group and this is an increasingly important way of booking rooms. Small, independent hotels without access to these systems will find that they come under increasing commercial pressure. There will be attempts to band together in associations so that small hotels are not excluded from this type of business.

Hotel chains also have one telephone number (such as Forte's 0800 40 40 40) which gives the consumer access to all of a company's hotels. Rather than the consumer ringing the individual establishment, the 'one-stop' number (especially when it is easily remembered) brings customer loyalty to the chain rather than the establishment. This type of approach particularly suits the busy business traveller, who can book a number of room nights in different hotels in one phone call.

This type of approach can be extended. Sheraton in the USA is experimenting with details on conference and meeting facilities available on a central computer. Conference and meeting planners in the USA contact Sheraton in Dallas through their computerized mail. The computer finds the hotel which matches their specific requirements. It is even possible to transmit images of the facilities available.

This type of approach assumes that the product is relatively standardized, with the consumer knowing what to expect, regardless of the location. The sales and marketing function shifts from the individual hotel to the regional sales team. The regional specialists can target particular companies, and follow through with leads that originally appeared at a local level. At the very least they can ensure that one hotel is not undercutting another in the chain. At best, the regional salespeople can ensure that the hotel chain successfully and profitably fulfils the needs of large client companies. Large, multinational hospitality corporations will use information technology to centralize this function more and more.

Links with a particular client company can build on the electronic links between the two companies. This might enable the business traveller to book his or her own rooms. It could also be used for settling the bills of all the company's travelling executives. The trend is for more and more information to be exchanged in computerized links.

Corporate headquarters can become a channel for communication from consumers, but they can also become a more efficient channel for communication within the company. This might mean the setting up of their own internal electronic mail system. Managers and operatives would simply type their memo into the computer, or take information direct from the screen, and send it to a computerized address. This has a number of advantages. First, the mail arrives (almost) instantly, though this is not the same as being read instantly. The computer has told the recipient that mail was waiting. Apart from saving forests it also means that the recipient can simply type in a response, and send it back to the originator. The same memo can be sent to a previously configured list of recipients all at the press of a button. As one Intercontinental manager put it: 'You don't even have to talk to them.'

Apart from convenience and speed, electronic mail is also highly accessible. The executive stuck in a hotel bedroom on one side of the world can be communicating through a laptop computer and modem with the executive offices which are still waiting for someone to arrive. The mail will be waiting in someone's computer when they arrive in the morning.

In fact, few hospitality corporations use electronic mail. Pringle in a 1993 survey of 115 hotels found e-mail in only seven of them. The strongly segmented culture of the hospitality industry means that there is very little motivation to improve communication between departments, let alone between hotels or between hotels and their head offices. If it is used at all there is a tendency to use it to 'fortress build' (interviewed systems manager). Productive use of e-mail remains concentrated on those managers who have to roam around as part of their job. A district manager in Gardner Merchant, for example, might use e-mail to get access to the secretarial facilities at central office. His or her letters could be printed on headed notepaper, and then sent out.

The centralized selling of a standardized product currently makes sense for a large corporation, but another impetus for the development of corporation-wide information systems is financial.

ACCOUNTANTS AS SYSTEM DESIGNERS

Head-office-based systems are also accounts-driven. First, the information that is transferred from the individual establishment to head office is mainly lists of figures. The existence of a chain implies the need for financial reporting. Money sent from the units to the centre has to be counted, and head office needs to manage its cash. Sometimes the centre can take that a step further with treasury management, which is where it uses its money to gamble on making more money, through investment or speculation.

This basic level involves the use of information technology. Head office accountants could be using Lotus-style spreadsheets to record and model operational data. They could be using software supplied by the banks through which they can monitor their own cash flow. Rather than wait for statements and then check the accuracy of the bank, financial information can be obtained through the accountant's PC-link with the bank's own records.

The main aim of the head office accountant is to provide regular profit and loss accounts, both for individual establishments and for the group. The speed with which these are produced are a function of the integration of various parts of the system. The De Vere group of hotels has its weekly returns collected automatically and these are translated into profit and loss accounts within two days. This is quite unusual for the hospitality industry: a product of the group's strongly standardized systems.

Apart from the provision of financial information, the central accountant wants to use this information for purposes of monitoring and control. At its simplest this can be a straightforward league table of profits. A more sophisticated approach is to develop budgets and then compare actual performance figures with those predicted in the budget. The target budgets are developed from past performance, with an allocation for inflation. In the past this would have been an onerously labour-intensive process, perhaps limited to once a year. With the accountant's use of information technology, it is possible to evaluate the performance of a hotel on a daily basis. Not only is this evaluation quicker, but it is also more detailed and the centre can use the technology to process far more detailed returns from the individual establishment.

The leisure industry is considerably more advanced with its corporate information systems than the hospitality industry. Here, the point of sales systems can be linked to the centre to provide overnight data on unit cash takings, sales analysis, staff performance and other control information. The corporate IT strategy 'will bring discipline' (corporate IT manager), not least on liquor inventory. A half a per cent improvement in gross profit could add £1 million to group profits; sorting out the cash till shortages could give £1 million extra profit to a large brewery.

With the technology available for very tight and detailed control of individual establishments, how the centre controls its units depends on the corporate philosophy. Fast-food franchise operations like McDonalds use technology to ensure a universally standardized product. Performance can be evaluated and compared throughout its global network. Ritzer (1993, p.101) has noted a 'shift away from control by people to control by technologies'. He notes that one of the reasons why fast-food restaurants have predominantly recruited teenagers is that they 'adjust more easily than adults to surrendering their autonomy to machines, rules and procedures'.

This is the automating side of information technology as used by large corporations. Pepsico, which owns KFC, Pizza Hut and Taco Bell, has a prototype for a machine that can produce a soft drink in 15 seconds. The computer receives the order and controls cup, ice, drink and lid. The drink is then transported to the customer on a conveyor belt, all complete with a smile. Rule number 17 for Burger King workers is 'Smile at all times'.

The manager is part of this process in the same way that the operative is locked into a rigid procedure. McDonalds managers have a set of manuals which laboriously detail the 'correct' course of action in any circumstance. The success of these manuals is measured by the extent to which they can cope with every eventuality. One result of this is Weber's 'irrationality of the rational'. McDonald's franchisees are forbidden to disseminate turnover figures, but they are perfectly happy to provide figures on the number of customers and average spend.

The McDonalds vision of information technology as the controlling medium of the multinational hospitality corporation dominates all sections of the British hospitality industry. When managers are asked for an example of a successful use of computers in their industry they tend to pick McDonalds, except for McDonald's managers who tend to pick Burger King.

However this not a vision shared by all hospitality companies – even the strongly branded ones. Scott's Hotels in the UK have used the last 17 years to move away from a strongly centralized approach. Monthly profit and loss accounts are the responsibility of the establishment's general manager. Establishment budgets are seen (by the centre) as a partnership between head office and the establishment, with the centre producing budget guidelines, such as inflation estimates.

The company has an overtly participative management style and the local general manager is seen as 'having ownership of the local decision-making process' (information systems director). Buchanan and McCalman's (1988) 'visibility theory' which was developed from a case study of a Scott hotel (mentioned in Chapter 5) probably owes more to the culture of this company, rather than the influence of information technology. In Scott's Hotels centre wishes become 'standards of operations', rather than directives. Even these 'standards' are compiled with the assistance of local general managers.

Scott's Hotels believe that their decentralized management style makes them more successful. Head office sees itself as support for the local hotels rather than as a controller, and information technology is a crucial part of this approach. Its application is consciously focused on the consumer, not so much the 'cutting edge of technology', but the 'cutting edge of customer services'. Investment is targeted where the customer will perceive an increase in quality. The success of this type of approach can only be judged by the company's long-term future.

THE ROLE OF KEY PEOPLE

One of the crucial influences on the degree of computerization for any company is its top executives. The software and hardware options the operative is using can often be traced back to the inclinations, priorities or prejudices of the chief executive. Scott's Hotels, mentioned above, have a board of directors which is strongly in favour of the application of information technology. Forte, on the other hand, has always displayed very mixed feelings about computerization at the top, and this has manifested itself throughout the chain, in its gradualist approach.

Often the influence from the top can come from outside this country. Daniels has shown that non-UK-owned companies generally are almost twice as likely to introduce advanced technological solutions in this country as their UK counterparts. This holds true for the hospitality industry as well. In part, this is probably caused by the relative success of pro-information technology companies. This gives them the opportunity to expand. However, part of the reason must be the increased emphasis that overseas ownership places on the need for non-face-to-face control. It's bad enough 'working out what your people are up to' in Norwich, 100 miles away, let alone when they speak another language and are 3,000 miles away.

For Scott's Hotels their Canadian owners were an important factor when deciding their IT strategy. Sometimes overseas ownership can impose a strict control on the establishment's hardware configuration, and the software packages that it uses. The phenomenon of software support being only an international phone call away, seems to be increasing for USA-owned hotels in London.

Corporate Hardware

Once upon a time (well, a couple of decades ago) computers filled huge rooms, cost the GDP of an Eastern European country, and needed teams of white-coated specialists to minister to them. These mainframes were the status symbols of the head offices of large multinational corporations. They were replaced by smaller computers known as minicomputers. Currently, the common model for the hospitality industry is the AS400 and this type of minicomputer is only affordable for head offices or very large hotels.

What really transformed the situation was the advent of the microcomputer, which for management is usually the personal computer (PC). These could be linked to the minicomputer, but they could also be linked to each other. Now costing less than an average month's wages, their speed and processing power has increased exponentially.

The debate in head offices about whether to choose micros linked to minis, or micros linked to each other, is ongoing. Most large hospitality corporations have adopted the AS400 route, and this has a number of significant implications. Not least is the expense, location and lack of flexibility of these systems. The historical trend is towards smaller, cheaper, more flexible computers – but this trend subtly undermines the concept of a head office.

In a sophisticated network of linked PCs, the marketing person could be working at home, with access to necessary information via his or her telephone line. The human resources manager is probably working on his laptop on the train at this moment, travelling to one of the hotels. The accountant is querying some figures with the bank and chasing for overdue weekly returns from a hotel. The difference is that he or she is working from home. They all need to get together to have a meeting? They use video conferencing, based on the cameras built into their computers.

Fantasy? Certainly at the moment in the hospitality industry. But the trend towards the 'virtual office' is increasing. People are more productive working from home, the corporate status symbol of the head office is expensive to run, information is not based upon piles of paper situated in space and time. All of these are reasons why the 'head office' is a concept that will increasingly be questioned.

Even the company itself is becoming a more amorphous collection. It does not just consist of salaried employees. What about the increasing use of people contracted in for a specific role, short-term contracts, the use of the self-employed for long periods? Are co-operating companies part of the same corporation? The 'virtual corporation' like the virtual office is making definitions increasingly fuzzy.

At present, head office is seen as the repository of information and skill, at least by the people at head office. By siting the minicomputers physically in the head office, managers are following a set of assumptions based on power relationships and the way in which they perceive their role. Effective use of information technology will gradually query these assumptions.

DEFINING SUCCESS

The head office vision of a successful implementation of information technology can have an impact on the way in which the managers perceive their role. New, microprocessor-based information systems do not just change the nature of the task, they change the nature of management itself.

If hospitality managers are asked how they define personal success or a 'job well done', they can use a number of criteria. They can see success in financial terms (the most common choice), or in terms of customer or staff satisfaction, operational factors, or their own internal, personal standards. However, a survey of 200 hospitality managers, found that just over one manager in 20 defined success as the perspective of their superior (Peacock, 1995). Performing your role successfully meant pleasing your boss, or at least minimizing the chances of the superior sacking you. These managers were well aware of the tension between this aim and any other definition of success: keeping your boss happy all the time is not exactly the same as putting all of your effort into ensuring the happiness of the customer. What it does represent is a (sometimes overtly) cynical career strategy for a large hospitality enterprise. People are not promoted on how well they perform a role, but on their superior's evaluation of their performance.

This type of superior-oriented manager is found in the large, chain hotels. They tended to be younger than average, and are over twice as likely to be male. All the managers who fell into this group worked for highly computerized establishments, and this was not true for any of the other groups of managers. Computerized establishments and hierarchically oriented managers appear to be linked. The computers serve to focus the attention of the establishment's managers on the needs of their superior. Most head offices might see this as a sign of success, but I have my doubts. There is a qualitative difference between serving the needs of customers and supplying head office with a perspective on how well the customer's needs have been met.

As computer systems are increasingly imposed by a centre striving to 'rationalize' its procedures and operations, one result will be an increase in the numbers of managers who define success as 'giving the impression at the strategic level of higher efficiency,' or 'making sure the general manager is not aware of any problems' (interview quotes). The attempts to 'rationalize' from the centre become the irrationality of individual manager's behaviour.

'BOTTOM UP' BUREAUCRATIZATION

One of the ironies of a tightly controlled bureaucratic approach to information systems is how this type of approach is always applied to those below the instigator in the corporate hierarchy, but rarely to their own level. Kroc's McDonalds is one of the most bureaucratic chain of establishments in the industry. Yet Kroc was a man who took his business decisions almost at the instinctive level. He was a creative and forceful business man, who would have found it impossible to work as the manager of one of his own establishments.

Most managers recognize that their job requires imaginative thinking, creativity, flair and flexibility. Yet, at the same time, what they want from people below them in the hierarchy is predictability, efficiency and calculability. 'Thus, the goal is to impose efficiency on subordinates, while those in charge remain as creative as possible'. (Ritzer, 1993, p.125).

The general manager of a large hospitality establishment could have a computer situated on his or her desk, but it is unlikely. If they do have their own personal computer, then they are probably part of an international chain and the computer is running standardized software chosen by corporate headquarters. In this situation the computer is possibly situated on a small table, just away from the main desk, or more probably in the assistant's office. The siting of the computer tells the observer about its significance and how it is used.

Corporate information systems are transforming the hospitality industry. New methods of selling, accounting, measuring, and communication are increasingly altering the working experience of hospitality managers. Yet at the same time what is driving this force is the corporate need to control its outlets. The dominant image is one of standardization, instant accountability and centralized control. On the informating/automating spectrum, very few companies pay even lip-service to the liberalizing force of the new technology. For the modern corporate executive, computers provide the comfort of 'knowing' the behaviour of branded establishments. The computer is seen as the tool to reduce the loneliness and isolation of the corporate executive.

An alternate vision is that as commercial power shifts from the point of control to the point of consumption, 'Head Office' will no longer be an external force directing and controlling local units, but a source of support and expertise, which can be called on at will by the local outlet. The centre becomes less a precise point in space and time, and more a series of information nets which contract and expand according to the issue or concern. The company itself becomes an 'open, networked, information-based organization' (Tapscott and Caston, 1993, p.61).

DISCUSSION TOPICS

Why did Kroc dislike using college graduates, at any level of his operation?

In the late 1980s, the international hotel section of THF (as it then was) started a drive towards decentralization and debureaucratization, organized by its new managing director, Alfonso Giannuzzi. What happened to it?

Does the hospitality industry need the manager who just does what he or she is told?

If the virtual corporation is a temporary collection of people and companies coming together for mutual advantage, what implications does this have for the loyalty of junior management?

7

Owners: The Mysterious Case of the VAT Man and the Bumbag

Underlying much of the discussion about the use of computers in the large hospitality company is the question of legitimacy or morality. The fiddling represented by the 'slippage' in head office's accounts is money that the centre feels has been stolen from it. For the unit manager, this 'slippage' could represent an extra payment to an operative for work beyond their normal duties. Sometimes, for an operative, theft can be perceived as an unofficial payment for the work they have done. The chef feels entitled to a lunch-time fillet steak because of those extra, last-minute customers that had to be catered for. Computer systems form part of the battle for control of these legitimate perks or unsanctioned theft (depending on your point of view).

For the owner of a small business the position is simple: the money belongs to him or her. For the owner the money is not a set of figures on a spreadsheet, it is a physical pile of money to be used at will. The only things threatening this relationship are the various revenue-collecting departments of the government.

Small companies dominate the hospitality industry, not just in terms of numbers of businesses, but also in terms of the proportion of total industry turnover. Large, multinational hospitality corporations are successful in acting as spokespeople for the industry, yet often their perspective represents a narrow, sectional interest. The small hospitality enterprise's owner-manager is not just a significant part of the hospitality industry, but in a number of ways he or she is the most innovative part.

A high proportion of hospitality businesses cease trading within the first year, yet they are constantly being replaced by a stream of newcomers. The success of the newcomers reflects their ability to adapt to changing markets, changing patterns of demand, changing tastes in restaurant wallpaper. The market is fostering a constant process of innovation. Long after the multinational hospitality corporation has fought a significant change through its board, the unsuccessful small hospitality manager has been replaced by an entrepreneur with a better product mix, the right price point or more aesthetically pleasing wallpaper. (Incidentally, it really is possible for boards of directors to discuss a decision as mundane as wallpaper.)

Even after the small hospitality business has been established it has a need to reshape itself. If it wishes to survive, it has to adapt to a constantly changing environment. Inability to change is linked to bankruptcy rates. The survivors demonstrate an ability to adapt in the face of changing patterns of demand. Those with a fixed concept of their product and service are much more likely to go to the wall, as their concept increasingly fails to match the expectations of prospective consumers.

The key player in this process is the owner-manager. When a business ceases trading, the owner tends to blame external factors: low consumer confidence, high interest rates, thieving or poor quality operatives. However, liquidators, who tend to be more objective, are much more likely to put the responsibility for the failure on the owner-manager: poor financial control, inability to adapt, lack of planning.

While the inexhaustible supply of new entrants to the industry, and the adaptability of the survivors, present a picture of change and innovation, one characteristic of the smaller firm in the hospitality industry is its reluctance to use information technology. We have seen in Chapter 6 how independent companies are over four times more likely than multiples to be uncomputerized. If you turn to size, and use a definition of size based on managers' own perspectives, then just over half of small hospitality establishments are uncomputerized. For large hospitality establishments, just over one in 20 are uncomputerized.

Even these figures can underestimate the gap between large and small. Some small hospitality establishments consider themselves computerized if their (hired-in) accountant is using a computer to process their accounts. The enterprise may have a sophisticated point of sales device, but they might use it in the same manner as an old fashioned till – albeit producing slightly more sophisticated bills. Overall there is little sense of information strategy forming a key part of the business concepts of owner-managers. On the whole, small, independent hospitality enterprises still tend not to use information technology.

This is not necessarily the case in other industries: sometimes it is the smaller enterprises which can make the most use of computers. Murray (1985) coined the term 'Benetton Economy' when discussing the loose network of independent, manufacturing and retail enterprises which lie behind that brand name. These small enterprises are characterized by their technological sophistication, which gives them a speed and flexibility that provides their competitive edge. The financial services industry has also felt the significance of the small, highly computerized establishment filling the niche market. The term 'design' is becoming synonymous with the computerized freelancer, when in the past it might have meant rows of shirt-sleeved men toiling over their drawing boards. Somehow the hotel and catering industry still seems divided between the computerized multiple and the uncomputerized small independent.

A number of reasons have been advanced for this divide. Some commentators suggest access to finance, with small businesses being unable to afford the cost of information technology. McCool (1986, p.54) found that the major manager-identified reason for the non-implementation of computerized management information systems was 'lack of capital', and owner-managers still identify this as the primary reason for not investing in computers.

In reality, a computer system could be purchased for around 2 per cent of annual sales, even for a two-person business. Leaving aside questions of leasing or credit arrangements, the purchase need not necessarily be a significant amount. Certainly a system could be purchased for less than half the cost of a commercial oven. Microcomputers are cheap, and more importantly they are getting cheaper. Owner-managers do not buy computer systems because they are too expensive, they decide not to purchase them because they consider that the advantages do not outweigh the cost.

How potential purchases are evaluated is a difficult area for the small business; rarely is it quantified. Sometimes the owner-manager sees the primary focus of any purchase is to reduce costs. In this respect the owner-manager is right not to purchase a system, as we have already seen that computer systems rarely reduce the numbers of staff.

Aside from the question of finance, Pine (1987, p.56) pointed to the advantage of standardization that the large multiple has: 'it is one of the requirements for technological development that a degree of standardization of operation prevails so that research and development activity can be properly resourced'. Leaving aside the issue of the large multiples that are not particularly standardized, research and development is not a significant feature of the large hospitality corporation. Essentially, products are purchased and adapted, even when subsequently rebadged as the corporation's own.

Another reason suggested for the gap between small and large hospitality concerns is the service sector effect. The belief that the use of information technology runs counter to the personal touch of a service industry is quite common in the smaller establishment. Blackman (1989) noted that just over one in ten surveyed hotel managers thought that computers were detrimental to customer service. However this proportion is declining and most owner-managers recognize ways in which IT can improve customer service.

Others point to the owner-managers themselves and suggest they lack the skills necessary to implement an IT strategy for the smaller hospitality business. Generally, the owner-manager of the small concern will not have qualifications above craft level, and McCool (1987) found that managers introducing computerized systems tended to be male graduates.

Certainly, educationalists adhere to this equation of qualifications, innovative managers and advanced, profitable technological solutions. However, there is no data to support it. It is true that graduates and diplomates in for example, Britain, tend to work in more computerized establishments, but this is because they tend to work for large hotel chains, which are more likely to use computers. There seems to be no causative link between qualifications and computer use, which says something about hospitality management education. It cannot be said that small hospitality businesses fail to use computers because their owner-managers are relatively less qualified.

It is worth pointing out also that a modern kitchen can be technologically sophisticated. Modern commercial microwave ovens, for example, can come complete with a wealth of sophistication hidden on their touch-sensitive screens. Technophobia is not a simple alternative explanation for the small business's reluctance to computerize.

To examine the reasons behind the low take-up of information technology in the small hospitality business sector you have to look at the personal characteristics of the owner-manager in detail. What type of person is an owner-manager? What are their motivations and ambitions? Suggesting that a lack of 'Will, finance and ability' (Whitaker 1987, p.231) are the reasons for the low take-up, is just another way of saying that the owner-manager doesn't want to use IT, doesn't think the benefits of IT are worth the expenditure, and is not prepared to spend time learning the necessary skills. Why not?

People starting their own hotel or restaurant businesses have a number of shared characteristics which differentiate them from other entrepreneurs. First, barriers of entry are quite low. A small business can be set up with a limited amount of capital, which is usually related to the entrepreneur's property. This is one of the reasons why catering is attractive to immigrants to this country. Often the business will also provide the owner-manager with accommodation, enabling them to sell their old property.

The skills required to set up this type of business are not perceived as a significant barrier of entry. Not only are there no restrictive qualifications, but most people feel that cooking and service skills are part of domestic existence and do not necessarily require further training. There is little in the way of effective government legislation which can hinder the process of setting up the hospitality business, for example in the way a garage has to register itself to carry out government safety checks. Relationships with suppliers are not constraining in the manner that newsagents are increasingly finding. Setting up your hospitality business may not be easy, but it is easier than establishing yourself in other industries.

The motivation for setting up in business may not be the desire for wealth. It has been suggested (Storey, 1994) that entrepreneurs tend to have had an unhappy childhood with difficulty relating to other children. Less esoterically, entrepreneurs are often looking to escape from something. It could be unemployment, or a role that they did not like, as Quinn, Larmour and McQuillan (1992, p.13) noted 'their previous jobs did not provide what they wanted'. Because of the low barriers of entry, this type of stimulus is much stronger in the hospitality industry than in other industries. The idea of owning your own restaurant, small hotel or bed and breakfast establishment has a charm which seems guaranteed to provide entrants to replace the thousands of bankrupts every year.

The desire of owners of small hospitality businesses for autonomy colours their business activities, often to the detriment of their business health. First, there is the question of investment. Owner-managers are loath to seek financing from the banks. Hankinson (1989, p.82) noted that his sample of small hotel owners 'seemed reluctant to take advantage of outside loans'. The owner-managers are even more reluctant to secure outside financing when it means that the bank might take an equity stake, that is, become a joint owner.

The commercial reality is that a considerable number of hospitality businesses go under because their are under-capitalized. They tend to lack operating capital for the initial start-up, when they are building up the levels of customers, and they have depleted their reserves with (always) unexpectedly high building costs. Some small hospitality businesses go under because the owner would prefer that to losing his or her autonomy.

Small business survival rates are linked with the entrepreneur's desire to expand the business. Businesses where the entrepreneur wants to remain the same size are much more likely to cease trading: it is difficult to tread water in business. Expansion will involve external finance, and we have already seen that the hospitality owner-manager is reluctant to secure this.

Next there is the question of outside advice. Successful entrepreneurs are generally characterized by a willingness to take advice from experts in their field. Yet, small hospitality enterprises generally do not actively seek specialist advice. Very few would use the free advice available from their local training and enterprise councils, and fewer still use outside consultancies – unless faced with a seemingly insoluble problem. The owner-manager exists in an individualist culture, with the metaphor of the ship's captain and choppy seas always cropping up in interviews. In my view, one reason why they sink so often is because they perceive the environment as hostile.

Next there is the question of remuneration. Entrepreneurs in the small business sector tend to have a fixed idea of the amount of money they should be taking out of the business. This is usually around 65–70 per cent of total profits. If the level of taxation on their income decreases, they tend to work less. If the level of profits drops, their income does not drop proportionally (Storey, 1994). If the business is doing well, then the consequence is likely to be an entrepreneur improving his or her golf handicap, rather than working on expanding the business further.

This attitude can extend into financial monitoring. For British industry as a whole, of all the businesses employing less than ten employees, only a third formally monitor profits (ibid.). Single-proprietor businesses, which make up the vast bulk of hospitality enterprises, are the least likely to hold information on paper or in the computer.

One owner-manager interviewed monitored business performance by the weight of notes and cheques which he carried in a bumbag belted to his waist. This provided him with a feeling of the relative profitability of each day: all he had to do was tap it and it supplied security and reassurance. He did not need a calculator, let alone an electronic point of sales system. The money was rarely counted, but simply distributed to suppliers or staff, the cheques were sent to the accountant. What was left in the bag at the end of the day was his.

Financial monitoring, or the lack of it, is inextricably linked to the black economy, or the entrepreneur's unofficial rake-off. Traditionally, the owner-manager of a small business 'conceals from his books part of what he deals in' (Mars, 1982, p.151). What he or she declares, he or she pays tax on. With VAT, income tax and national insurance, a high proportion of money has gone, even before the establishment starts making a profit.

The black economy is particularly significant for the hospitality industry because of the large proportions of cash transactions. Cash, providing it does not go through a bank account, provides an untraceable form of income which the taxation authorities can only estimate. The hospitality industry is one of the last industries where an establishment can insist that payment is made in cash. Sometimes the volume of trade is such that it is impractical to use anything else.

Within the hospitality industry there is a divide on this issue between small and large hospitality businesses. In research the author found that one in eight managers in large establishments consider that tax avoidance plays a part in the low take-up of information technology. The figure was one in four for small establishments. Whereas managers of large, multinational hospitality corporations can be irritated by the implication of tax evasion, owner-managers see it as a regular feature of the industry.

During the interview with the owner-manager with the bumbag, one of his chefs came up to him and was paid with cash from the bag. Not only does this free the owner from employers' official obligations and state contributions, but the fact that the wage is tax-free can reduce the total wages bill. He does not have to pay the chef as much as if the wage was taxed. If the chef is claiming 'jobseeker's allowance' or other state support, then that too will, in effect, act as a subsidy to a level of wages which is lower than it might otherwise be. Although managers can talk of 'cowboys' in the industry, with implications of unqualified, sloppy or illegal activities, these practices are widespread among small hospitality businesses. Without them there would be a reduced incentive for the entrepreneur to risk his or her investments, house, to create jobs and service customer needs. The only real surprise was the relative openness of the bumbag transactions.

If you take these factors together, the puzzle is not the low take-up of information technology in the hospitality industry. What is more surprising is that *anyone* uses a computer in their small hospitality business.

First, the hospitality entrepreneur's desire for autonomy clashes with the McDonalds-style image of computer use. We have already seen how this emphasizes central control and predictability. This is what the owner-manager wants to get away from. It is an attitude not confined to small business owners. Once I saw the chief executive of a large contract catering company offer a management job to someone who had just dropped a computer, on the grounds that: 'Anyone who knows how to treat computers can have a job in my company any day.' This is a company which I have used in this book as an example of good practice, but I still think it is unlikely that this chief executive has a computer on his desk.

The owner-manager's desire for autonomy does not extend to his or her own operatives. We have already noted the hospitality industry's authoritarian and hierarchical tendencies. The authoritarian tendencies are even more marked in the small hotel and in restaurants. Small hospitality establishments have managers who are almost three times more likely to identify their management style as autocratic and half as likely to be democratic, when compared to large establishments (Peacock, 1994c).

Whereas the autocratic hospitality corporation needs computer systems to control its operations, the autocratic owner-manager is on-site directly overseeing his or her operatives. The owner may sit in a corner constantly watching his or her staff, or may see his or her role as controlling the billing process. Any concept of information technology as a co-operative process will clash with the management style of an owner like this. These owners are more concerned by the idea of staff fiddles, as they take it personally: it's their money. After all, they probably worked as operatives and they are aware of the potential for theft.

Traditional under-financing is also going to work against the use of computers. After the owner has overspent on what he or she considers essential (expensive carpets, copper pans), the money has run out and the owner is unwilling to seek additional finance. The owner of a small hospitality business perceives investment differently to a manager in a large corporation. It is seen much more in terms of 'the money available' or 'replacing obsolete equipment', rather than in the effect the investment could potentially have on cost reduction, increasing profits or operational efficiency. In another study (Peacock, 1995), managers were asked to cite their primary reason for investment, and while 'money available' or 'replacing equipment' (need) could be linked to costs and profits, the primary focus of the respondents demonstrated a difference in approaches, as shown in Table 7.1.

Table 7.1 Cited reasons for investment in hospitality establishments (figures expressed as a percentage of the sample)

	Money available	Need	Profit	Operational	Cost
Large	16	18	18	13	11
Small	30	21	14	7	5

Those managers who saw investment decisions as part of a desire to control costs had the highest productivity (expressed as average sales for each employee) of any group. This was also the group with the lowest proportion of small businesses. Not only does the lack of finance restrict the small hospitality business's opportunities to invest in information technology, but the way in which investment is perceived also works against IT and against the health of the business.

The hospitality owner-manager's sense of individualism also works against the use of information technology. He or she sees the business as a relationship between its customers and the establishment. There is little sense of a group of establishments competing for the same group of customers. Consequently there is little in the way of monitoring of the competition. This is true for the industry as a whole, but is particularly true for the small sector. Owner-managers are not just resistant to advice, they are, in the main, resistant to anything from the external environment impinging on their business.

Behind the resistance to investment, advice and competition monitoring is this question of the entrepreneur's income. Economists often make the assumption that a business is trying to maximize its profits. Yet, hospitality owner-managers are attempting to secure a target level of income. Any increases in profitability over the target figure can lead to a reduced interest in the business. Theoretically, an income below target could lead to a strong interest in cost-reduction and profit-maximizing strategies, but at this point the establishment is in trouble and there is little cash available for investment, even if the entrepreneur is willing to envisage it.

This equivocal stance towards profit maximization is also linked to the low formal monitoring of accounts. A commodity the hospitality owner-manager is always short of is time, and financial monitoring receives a low priority. When there is little financial control on paper, why should a computer be purchased?

Low formal monitoring is not just linked to mixed attitudes to profit maximization, it is also linked to the unofficial economy. One image of IT that interviewed owner-managers sometimes mentioned was computers being carried out of the offices of an allegedly misbehaving company. Customs and Excise in the UK, have significant powers when it comes to VAT investigations. In a raid that I observed personally a few years ago, I was impressed with the fear they could produce in the owner-manager, who they had just dragged out of bed.

It is at this point that the restaurant or hotel owner does not want the financial affairs of the establishment to become instantly visible by the government official switching on the computer. The entrepreneur might be willing to tolerate a little financial fuzziness, so as not to risk total transparency.

FUTURE PROSPECTS

We have examined some of the characteristics of the hospitality owner-manager and looked at how these characteristics relate to the low take-up of information technology. How will this situation change? In the past, the owner-manager would have disputed the link between computers and customer service, but this is a dwindling group of entrepreneurs.

The key question is the financial monitoring: 'The more successful firms are those which keep and use financial data with which to make key business decisions' (Storey, 1994, p.311). At the moment most restaurant entrepreneurs have only the vaguest idea of business performance, with perhaps a monthly kitchen percentage figure, showing the proportion of sales that food costs leave. There is rarely any detailed breakdown for each menu item, other than an initial pre-costing, and rarely any analysis of figures against time.

The entrepreneur is vulnerable, not just to pilfering, but to changes in cost structures, sudden changes in patterns of demand, even seasonal variations. It is the detailed provision and use of this type of information which can enable the entrepreneur to survive. Even if the information needs are unchanged, an information system can ensure the more timely production of figures, e.g. the monthly sales analysis becoming a weekly one. A comprehensive information system could also help the successful entrepreneur find the time for his or her leisure activities: a fully informed golf-player.

Built-in flexibility, which the successful business needs and the information system facilitates, is never going to be easy for a product/service-centred small hospitality establishment. Most establishments of this type rely on very cheap (often family) labour, and poorly rewarded entrepreneurs, who are sometimes merely comparing their income with benefit levels, rather than other entrepreneurs' incomes. It would seem likely that this group will be unwilling and unable to reprioritize information technology for some time.

Even for the entrepreneur who seeks a certain level of income, rather than profit maximization, it could be argued that an initial commitment to the role of information-gathering and technology could help. More training might overcome this resistance to financial monitoring, but the individualist culture means the entrepreneur is unwilling to receive this training. Government business training initiatives in Britain for example, have had a conspicuous lack of success. The training itself can be of questionable value. Storey (1994) noted that business success rates are not related to training, but that there is a correlation between the entrepreneur's general education and business survival.

Although there is a link between undeclared income and the low usage of computers at the moment, this will change. The traditional recourse of the entrepreneur wishing to avoid meeting his or her obligations, was two sets of books. An accurate set and a set for tax collecting agencies. For the time-constrained, non-monitoring hospitality entrepreneur this would be a major undertaking. However, adjusted sets of accounts are a very simple process on a computer. The accounts file/system is copied and key adjustments made to the copy.

I have seen systems where a number of parallel systems are automatically kept up to date by the computer, using the truthful files as a base and then making pre-programmed adjustments. A set for the bank, for when you want to apply for extra loans, a set for the VAT people, a set for head office and even a truthful set. All of these printed out at the press of a button (or two). Manipulation of information is the basis of a computer system, and as this is increasingly appreciated by an income-maximizing hospitality entrepreneur, this will overcome the fear of the computer being carried out by tax-collecting officials. After all, if the worst comes to the worst, a file is easier to dispose of than a set of account books.

SUMMARY

Gradually, computers will become more widely used in the small hospitality enterprise. In the same way that owner-managers no longer generally see information technology as a threat to their concept of service, other fears about computers (e.g. making their finances transparent) will disappear. Yet at the same time there will not be a tidal-wave of computerized hospitality businesses, in the way in which we have seen financial services transformed.

What is stopping this process is the individualistic culture of the owner-manager: his or her vision of the ship's captain in the storm of consumer behaviour. This image is highly unlikely to change. This culture means that the owner-manager is not going to monitor the competition, seek external advice, find outside sources of finance or follow new developments in the industry. The culture will also emphasize the direct control of operatives. The direct result of this will be an entrepreneur who does not see any relevance in the application of information technology.

At the speculative level it could be suggested that small hospitality enterprises are linked with a patriarchal culture. There does appear to be a link between small business culture and the cultural prominence of central male figures. In Britain, ethnic minorities such as Greek Cypriots demonstrate well above average rates of business ownership. Yet this culture places a lot of significance on the role and power of the father. Women play a supporting role, not just in the business itself, but in the domestic servicing of the male 'entrepreneur'. Other cultures can show the same characteristics. Many Indian restaurants are run by Bengalis, who have a very limited restaurant culture of their own. Bengali cuisine is essentially domestic, that is, cooked by women. Yet women chefs are exceptionally rare in Indian restaurants. The same could be said of Chinese restaurants, where there is a distinct social pressure against women working in professional kitchens.

Even in ethnic groups where women play a more prominent role, such as British, white, Anglo-Saxon protestants, women make up well under half of small business owners. Part of this relationship between central male figures and hospitality business ownership may be linked to the role of inheritances. If a relatively well-off family figure dies, the money, or the business, could be divided equally between all the siblings. However, in a more patriarchal culture there is a tendency for the oldest male to inherit the larger portion (if not all) of an inheritance. Inherited wealth plays a significant role in business creation, and an even more prominent role in business ownership.

Part of the reason why an entrepreneur may devote a considerable part of their life to a business may be the desire to see the business (and their name) live on after their demise, a kind of life after death. To this end, they do not want to see the business sold and divided, they want an offspring (usually a son) to take on the business and make it grow.

If the successful small hospitality business is linked to the cultural importance of a powerful, central, male figure, it could help to explain the non-cooperative style of this type of enterprise. Perhaps as the proportion of women restaurant and hotel owners increases, management style in the industry will move away from the directive and authoritarian. In the long term this could have a profoundly significant effect on the use of information technology. We shall have to wait and see.

DISCUSSION TOPICS

Is tax evasion a more serious crime than staff pilfering?

Does the reduction of taxes on income produce more work or less?

How might you motivate hospitality entrepreneurs to work harder?

Is maleness linked to an autocratic and non-consensual style of management?

8

Studies: Computers – Absent or in Action

WAGAMAMA

Situated near to the British Museum in central London, Wagamama is conscious of its position at the fashionable edge of English eating. A British operation which opened in 1992, it serves Japanese fast food, predominantly noodles dishes, offering a healthy style of eating to a young clientele. The prices are not particularly expensive, with a noodle dish costing around £5. The setting is functional, with a great deal of wood and shared seating, combined with a spartan 1990s designer feel. Rather Scandinavian in style. The place is highly successful, and most times it is necessary to queue to get in. There are plans for new versions of Wagamama.

Wagamama uses information technology in all aspects of its operation. Most notable for the customer are the hand-held terminals used by the waiters to take orders. The system chosen was a Remanco one, and Pegasus accounting software is also used, with data transferred to Pegasus manually. The Remanco system cost approximately £35,000 and there is a £700 monthly maintenance fee.

The food servers' hand-held devices enable the server to tap in the order, which is then transmitted (after a check with the customer) via radio waves, to a printer in the bar or kitchen. There are occasional breakdowns, when the restaurant is forced to use manual systems, and these breakdowns create significant problems for the management. At Smolensky's in the Strand, also in central London, where a similar system is used, managers believed that the high proportion of mirrors on the walls in the restaurant produced breakdowns.

The main function of the Remanco system is to improve speed of service ('automate the customer'). At Wagamama, on average the customer queues for 20 minutes before sitting down, drinks (e.g. 'raw juice') can be ordered while waiting. Drinks are served within two minutes of the customer sitting and the food is served between eight and ten minutes after sitting. Because of the pressure of newly arriving customers, this is not a place to linger over your meal. In the jargon of the menu, Wagamama is referred to as a 'non-destination food station': somewhere to eat quickly when you are going on somewhere else. 'Good value and lingering over meals are, unfortunately, not compatible' (the menu). One interesting feature of this sort of technology is that sometimes, if the restaurant were not busy, the server could deliberately delay the arrival of the food to give the customer a more relaxed meal. Because the food servers do not have to go into the kitchen to hand over their orders, they can spend more time in the restaurant, either taking orders or interacting with customers. The food servers nevertheless process a high number of customers.

The cashier's terminal incorporates and analyses a vast amount of sales data. Detailed bills are produced quickly, and the cash is speedily and securely handled. A vast amount of information is held on the system, including revenue statistics, sales analysis, labour costs, server productivity and profitability.

Looking at the management style of the establishment, Wagamama is highly unusual in hospitality industry terms. The restaurant uses a Japanese management philosophy termed 'Kaizen'. Kaizen means continual improvement and stresses the active involvement of everyone in the running of the establishment and the suggesting of improvements. Unlike most restaurants, the managers dress similarly to the operatives, and there is a continual emphasis on staff consultation and feedback. Decision-making is seen as a collective activity.

Part of the unusually collective feel of the establishment can be put down to the similarity of ages. Staff and managers are exceptionally young, with an average age of food servers of around 20, while managers average 24 and the owner is 32. Wagamama's management equates youth with a more positive and flexible attitude to new technology, but we have already seen how age is not necessarily a factor when it comes to technophobia. It seems more realistic to suggest that the youthfulness of the operatives reflects the availability of student labour and a desire to present a youth culture that matches the target market. It is difficult to imagine 50-year-old food servers at Wagamama.

Wagamama operatives are happy with the technology they are using. Apart from reservations about the odd technical hiccup, they find it accessible and useful. When asked which animal they would choose if they were to describe technology in terms of animals, they tended to name domestic pets such as cats and dogs. It would be difficult to suggest from this that they find information technology alienating and threatening.

Oddly enough this contrasts with a difference of attitude on the part of Wagamama's management. In conversation, managers would be positive about the systems. However when they were asked about the animal that they would use to describe their system, they were likely to name animals like lions and tigers. There are a number of possible explanations. It could be down to technical problems, or the high initial investment and maintenance charges. Certainly managers named the computer system as the biggest risk that they had taken in the business.

The managers' hidden reservations about the system could also be caused by the problems (needing solutions) which the information on the systems suggested. However, Wagamama's managers remain committed to information technology. They could not imagine running the restaurant without the system (at least, not on a regular basis) and they wanted to invest in more sophisticated systems increasingly tailored to their needs.

What is particularly interesting about Wagamama is that it is large (70 staff, including part-timers) and independent. The tendency within the hospitality industry for hotels to be more computerized than non-hotels, and for multiples to be more computerized than independents has already been noted. Wagamama is one of a small, but growing, number of large independent restaurants that buck the trend. These establishments are more likely to be computerized than large independent hotels, and are more likely to be computerized than large chain restaurants.

Newly established innovative restaurants appear to be building in creative applications of information technology from the beginning. Another example would be Belgo, the Belgian restaurant in north-west London which specializes in mussels, chips and Belgian beer. An interesting feature of these places is that often they are established and run by people who have not traditionally devoted their careers to the hospitality industry. Because they are trying to break established patterns they appear to favour people from outside the industry.

There is no doubting Wagamama's success. From the queues, satisfied customers and the plans for expansion, the formula can be seen to be working. The average member of staff at Wagamama generates sales of £10,000 a year more than the average hospitality worker, but the average spend is the same as in a pizza restaurant. Essentially, Wagamama is McDonalds for a niche market: high-volume, short-stay business, low-cost, standardized product, with a strong emphasis on technology to control the operation.

One of the key features of their success is the management philosophy. There are some managers who see themselves as autocratic, and their operatives agree. However, in contrast to McDonalds, there is a significantly more co-operative ethos overall, which fosters the effective use of the technology and provides a flexibility and resilience which gives the establishment its strength.

TOKYO DINER

Sometimes it appears that in our *Bladerunner* style future, we'll all be eating Japanese noodles – even if they are only Pot Noodles. They're cheap, healthy and tend to be vegetarian, so can claim to be more ethical: an unstoppable combination. The cheaper Japanese restaurants represent more than a passing London fashion, they are an increasing trend.

The Tokyo Diner, near to Leicester Square, in London's West End, follows in the Wagamama tradition of cheap Japanese food, served to a younger target market. Again it is a successful formula, quite often complete with queues. The main difference from Wagamama is the scale, it is a much smaller restaurant, but growing. For a small restaurant it is highly computerized, with a sophisticated point of sales system. Orders are taken manually and printed out in the kitchen, a detailed bill is left on the table, and you pay on exiting the restaurant.

The system used is a Kar Corporation one, and unlike the Wagamama system it is not that obvious to the customer. As a point of sales device it has a lower profile and makes less noise than a conventional till. The owner-manager can monitor sales from his position by the door. The restaurant and kitchen can monitor each other through the use of video cameras. One interesting feature of such a sophisticated system is that payment must be in cash. Cheques, debit cards and credit cards are not accepted.

The system is used by the owner-manager both to monitor the business performance of the establishment and to speed up the turnover on tables. There are fewer errors on billing and the customer receives a detailed, itemized bill, while the chef gets a detailed printout. Compared with more traditional, rival restaurants, the owner-manager has shifted from a highly priced, low-volume product, to a low-price, high-volume one. His product is more competitive, yet at the same time it is necessary to monitor his margins to ensure that he makes the required degree of profit. Information technology plays a key role in all this, was built into the restaurant from the start, and the owner-manager remains committed to enhancing this area of the business. With the high concentration of restaurants around Leicester Square (especially Chinatown), information technology provides Tokyo Diner with a competitive edge. As the eating out habit grows, and customers become more fickle and mobile, this is a trend that can only continue.

The owner, an ex-pilot, uses the language of the automator when he talks of wanting 'the restaurant to run like a plane'. Yet at the same time there are highly unusual attributes for a small restaurant. Not least is the bonus scheme for operatives which is based on gross profit margins. Most restaurants would find this difficult simply on the grounds that the necessary information was not readily available.

It might be thought that Tokyo Diner and Wagamama use information technology because it fits their modern, high-tech, Japanese image. More traditional restaurants might find the idea of remote order pads for their waiters more disconcerting: what Maureen Lipman once called in a letter to an example of this type of establishment as the 'nuns in g-strings' effect. Certainly the perceptions of customers are important. On the fifth floor of Harvey Nichols in Knightsbridge, the brasserie operation has waiters using hand-held devices, while the more up-market restaurant on the same floor has waiters using pen and paper.

Tokyo Diner does exhibit a love of gimmickry, with taps that sense the hand underneath and do not have to be turned on, and the touch-sensitive sliding door. However, the point of sales system is discreet and would not be out of place in any small restaurant. Less significant than the Japanese food that they both serve is the fact that both these restaurants are new, and successful.

CUMBERLAND HOTEL

The Cumberland Hotel is a large, 900-roomed hotel, situated in central London by Marble Arch. It is owned by Forte and is very busy, with occupancy ratings usually well above 90 per cent. Its 360 full-time staff is actually quite small for a hotel of this size, giving average sales per employee figures of over £60,000 a year. All of this makes for a very profitable hotel.

The Cumberland uses a number of different systems, but we shall look specifically at the reservations side of the operation. A few years ago the hotel was using the Datahost system as its property management system, but this was changed in 1992 to the Carahost system. Although purchased outside the company, the original system had been constantly adapted and altered to fit the needs of the company. One adaptation was necessary simply to enable the package to cope with the Cumberland Hotel's large number of rooms. The hotel has fibre optic cabling linking it to the central reservation system used by Forte's divisional computer services department.

The new reservations system brought with it a number of improvements over the old one. Occupancy figures have always been high, but there was an increase in revenue with a higher yield: shifting the business to higher rates. The new system was much quicker at processing a reservation: it now takes from one to five minutes depending on the complexity of the booking. Whereas the old system meant that quite often information had to be looked up on paper, Carahost put more information, such as room rates, on the screen, for immediate access. Both supervisors and operatives found the new system a considerable improvement.

That is not to say that the operation of the new system is perfect. Occasionally (about twice a year) the system 'goes down' and once about 80 'ghost rooms' appeared on the system, leading to much confusion. On the whole these technical problems are minor, and represent a considerable improvement on the old system.

A more significant set of problems is linked to the hierarchical style of the company. Information technology is a process that is strictly controlled from the centre. The systems that are used by the Cumberland are imposed at Forte's divisional level and this would include decisions to upgrade from Datahost to Carahost. Nominally there is some independence at the local level for enhancements and improvements to the system. However, because of controls on the budget held by the centre, systems are rarely adapted at the local level to suit the specific needs of the hotel.

Forte grew mainly from the acquisition of other companies. These companies each had their own philosophies and distinctive ways of working. Managers and operatives in acquired companies would not always feel their first loyalty to (what was then) THF. It is easy to see how this would lead automatically to strong centralizing tendencies. The companies had to be moulded into one collective entity and this had to be done by the centre.

To an outsider an interesting feature of the Forte organization above local level is its closedness. You are passed from one person to the next, questions must be submitted in writing and overall there is this feeling of resistance to exploration. With other companies it can be different. Often they are surprised about your interest, but usually after you start talking, a certain amount of pride can creep into their descriptions of their work. Not once have I had that experience in interviewing Forte personnel.

This is not just the whinging of a researcher, it is indicative of a deeply held company philosophy. One interviewed graduate who had been working at the Cumberland for just under a year, expressed frustration at the limited knowledge he was allowed to gain in his job. Reservation operatives felt that they were 'informed', but felt that because they were 'kept under strict control' they were given little time to experiment with the system. If this sounds like a minor consideration, it should be noted that this is how people learn about their jobs. Even the rooms manager said that he had learned most by 'trial and error'.

Reservation operatives are strictly controlled, with a considerable emphasis being put on reducing their access to the complete system, through the use of authorization codes. One operative was asked to represent how she saw herself in relation to the company with a picture. She drew a tiny dot in the middle of an A4-sized piece of paper. It was a succinctly graphic illustration of the extent of her alienation from her work.

One manager of my acquaintance went for an interview as a reservations manager with a sister hotel to the Cumberland. At the interview she talked of working with staff, fostering co-operation and leading by example. All quite standard procedure for the Marriott hotel that she had worked in before. She was rejected on the grounds that it was necessary to control staff tightly and to tell them what to do. There was clearly a clash of cultures between the two chains.

Information technology generally leads to more control over their jobs for operatives. More information is available, more sophisticated techniques can be used and routine tasks are speeded up. However, at the Cumberland Hotel the reservations staff felt that, increasingly, information technology gave them less control over how they did their jobs. The automating aspects of the technology were emphasized to the point of extreme alienation. When a reservations operative was asked what would she say to her terminal if it were a human she responded: 'Can we do something else today?'

The picture is not one of a group of operatives who would just like to do less work, but of a group looking for a different way of working, who are actively seeking to become more involved in their tasks and the management of them. The fact that they are not succeeding is directly attributable to the corporate culture of the company, expressed by the centre. When asking at divisional level whether staff were consulted on improvements to the system, the response was: 'Yes, for minor and cosmetic changes.' In other words, as long as it does not make a real difference. Although Rocco Forte can claim 'Today, systems development is operator driven' (Teare and Boer, 1991, p.6), this is not the experience of managers and operatives at the local level.

When asked for their definition of the purpose of information technology the response from divisional staff was: 'tactical business initiatives', which is a deliberately limited response. Most large, multinational companies would talk about the strategic value of information technology, Forte is talking about the tactical value. Yet at the same time the centre is being criticized for its lack of support for its own systems: 'I do not think that they know enough about the system' (Cumberland manager on central software support). Criticisms of software support lines are quite rare, although some companies appear to limit support for older versions of their products. Forte's centre is being criticized for the support of a product which it helped develop and install at the Cumberland.

Forte is not anti-technology. It is putting considerable effort into some information technology projects. The new, company-wide reservation package (Fortres II) represents a considerable investment and is much faster and more efficient than its predecessor. The problem is simply that these projects are being implemented through a culture that emphasizes central control.

The Cumberland Hotel is a working formula, so it appears churlish to criticize it in business terms. It is possible that the authoritarian culture produces the required volume of business for lower levels of staff numbers and staff wages. On the other hand, when talking to guests about their perception of the Cumberland, if their opinions could be summarized in one word it would be 'efficient'. However, when the same guests were asked what they were looking for in a hotel, the word summarizing their views was 'friendly'.

Reservations operatives too, valued personal communication with guests, but felt constrained by their role into minimizing this communication. Perhaps when Cumberland Hotel managers are seeking marginal improvements to increase their yield even more, the better approach might favour the use of technology to foster individual initiative and personal contact between guest and operative. With eight reservations operatives and a turnover of £23.5 million, one operative really can make a difference.

GARDNER MERCHANT

Let us now examine the use of computers by Gardner Merchant's client account executives (district managers). These are managers responsible for a number of different units. They sit uneasily between unit management, the client who pays Gardner Merchant and the centre, represented by regional office.

Relatively recently these executives have been equipped with laptop computers, complete with modems which can link the manager with other sections of their organization. These laptops come complete with a series of Lotus spreadsheets, designed by the centre, which can be used, altered and restructured by the account executive. A specialist client report can be produced on site, quickly. Costs such as National Insurance and other employee commitments, can be calculated automatically. As well as speed and flexibility the process is more transparent. Charges incurred by the client, such as training, can be clearly shown. This helps to build trust with the client. Costs, even for a cup of tea, can be broken down in detail and a production contingency can be built in for overportioning or wastage.

The accessibility and detail of the laptop spreadsheets can greatly assist the job of the executive. Budgets are initially developed by the unit managers, but relating actual performance to budget is the job of the account executive. Sometimes the budget that the unit manager is working on need not necessarily be the same for the client. The account executive needs leeway for errors and disasters.

Another key problem for a contract catering company is cash flow. The client has 30 days in which to pay, but any delay in presenting the monthly invoice can result in a 'negative cash situation'. Staff and other bills have to be paid before the client pays the bill. Use of IT means that the client will receive the invoice just over a week after the books are closed. This is a gap which is narrowing.

I have mentioned Gardner Merchant's e-mail system before, but there are a couple of interesting features of the diary that accompanies it. First, appointments and movements are visible to anyone who accesses the diary. Second, it used to be possible to book appointments for other executives, but this ran into problems.

Gardner Merchant have a number of central, mainframe systems. GAMBIT is their trading and invoicing system. Account executives can access this through their laptops and make changes to budgets. They also have a debt collecting system, called OLAS, and their sales and marketing system is called MIDAS. Their file transfer utility is particularly useful for the client account executive. Headed notepaper is controlled at the centre and any letters that the executive produces can be completed on site, printed out at the regional offices, and posted from there.

Overall, the area managers recognize a strong board-down stress on information technology. It is intended that more of the catering units themselves will have their own computers, mainly for food and beverage control systems. Here the emphasis is very much on centralized control. One area manager suggested that one justification for this might be to force a unit to use a particular supplier every week. A return of zero for that supplier would mean that the unit would be included on an exception report, and be made accountable for the failure.

Account executives are much more flexible than this. The use of spreadsheets on laptops gives them an adaptability and speed of response, which can emphasize the imaginative solving of problems. These executives are assessed (by regional superiors) on their performance every month. The laptop systems mean that they can spend more time with local units, can access information more quickly and respond faster. They seemed agreed that the worst feature of the system was physically carrying the laptop. Consciously or not, Gardner Merchant has shifted the IT emphasis away from strongly centralized systems to more local flexibility.

MR D'S SNACK BAR

Mr D's snack bar is part of a small chain in Kent in south-east England. There is nothing very unusual about this establishment, it is fairly typical of a large range of non-users of IT. The snack bar's three full-time staff and one part-timer have a turnover of just under £70,000. This is not much more than the Cumberland Hotel's average sales for each member of staff.

Although the manager of the establishment quite likes the idea of computers, the owner of the chain is adamant that computers represent a 'waste of money'. Profits are unchanged over the last six months and there is little cash available for investment. Both the manager and the owner agree that the establishment simply can't afford it.

The owner takes an active part in the operation of his establishments, but undertakes little in the way of formal monitoring and control. Very little financial data is written down. The manager and owner are linked by a common ethnic background (Turkish Cypriot) and there are kinship ties which help to reinforce feelings of loyalty. Expectations are also low, and neither the manager nor the owner perceive their turnover as low for the size of the establishment. Attitudes to government revenue-collecting bodies can only be described as antagonistic. The manager and owner have strong feelings of isolation. Their ethnic origin means a feeling of separation from the main community, and this is increased by their unsocial hours.

BAR GANSA

Sometimes the link between control and the use of a system can be even more explicit. Bar Gansa is a busy Spanish-style restaurant in Camden, North London. With 20 employees and an annual turnover reported on a survey undertaken in 1994, as being £500,000, productivity seems a little low for such a successful restaurant. However, it is possible that the £500,000 quoted represents some rounding of figures. Awareness of turnover figures (or the willingness to give precise ones) seems related to the use of computer systems. Figures provided to the nearest thousand pounds came from highly computerized establishments, who tended to have large turnovers. On one memorable occasion I was provided with figures to the nearest penny.

Bar Gansa was not using IT and this was related to the attitude of the British owner: 'The present system works efficiently. However, if I was less involved in the day-to-day running, I would definitely consider it.' In fact, the owner had investigated possible systems, looking particularly at the Remanco system. The possible purchase of a system was related to the question of the owner moving away from direct personal control of the establishment. This was a clear indication of the link between how the owner chooses to exercise control and whether (and how) a computer system is used.

Although the establishment had increasing profits in the six months prior to the interview, the desire to increase the surplus was not necessarily the primary drive for the owner. When asked how he determined his success, he responded by talking about 'contented staff' and 'not working when I shut the door at night'. Certainly, to see the restaurant as an exercise in profit maximization is too simplistic.

EYNE HOUSE

Situated near Snowdonia in Wales, Eyne House is a large house with outstanding views and six guest bedrooms. The owners, a couple, run the business as a bed and breakfast establishment, though it is possible to arrange to have evening meals there as well. Rooms are individually furnished with antique furniture and the establishment prides itself on the quality of its food.

Originally the business began as a lifestyle choice, with the family leaving London for a rural environment. The house was purchased with redundancy money. Turnover is exceptionally low, especially when you take into account the fact that the children act as (unpaid) operatives. On the other hand, with food and accommodation provided, in effect, free to the owners, this can offset the lack of profits.

Both owners were used to using computers in their previous business existences and built them into the operation of the house from the beginning. Bookings are kept on a spreadsheet, with details of advanced payments and deposits. Originally this was used to produce bills, but the owners found that it was too formal, and a much more informal handwritten bill is now used. When a potential guest rings up to book, the owners imply that they are looking up the details in a book, and they only type in the handwritten details of the booking after the guest has rung off. The owners feel that the clattering keyboard clashes with the log-fire and Aga ambience that they work so hard to create.

With records of previous bookings on the computer, together with charges, the owners were able to use this information to adjust charges. Their business is intensely seasonal, and they have used the information on the computer to increase the seasonal difference in their charges, and they have used the computer to quantify consumer response to price changes, related to season. In effect, they are using the computer for elementary yield management.

As well as bookings, accounts are kept on the computer. There is also a guest history system stored on a database. This records the details of the guest, including his or her address, what room they stayed in, how the guest heard about the establishment and even a code for type of customer (it includes one for 'dirty weekend'). Their coding system has become more sophisticated with age. Originally they had a code for 'walker', which is now divided into 'rambler', 'hill walker' and 'climber'.

The house prides itself on the personal touch with the guests becoming aware of the establishment through word of mouth. There is a lot of repeat business and the owners have developed a prodigious memory of names and faces. However, this word of mouth is given a regular prod. First, there is a follow-up letter after the stay, produced by the word processor automatically taking details from the customer database. Second, there is a newsletter which gives details of the house and events in the local area. The content of this little newsletter varies according to the type of customer, and it is timed to coincide with the guest making their holiday decisions. The process sounds complicated, but it is largely automated. The main task for the owners is inputting the guest history details.

The guest history database is now being used to experiment with special promotions designed to fill the bedrooms during slack periods. One of the aims of the owners is to compact demand, so that they can extend their own winter break (in the sun) without loss of income: certainly not profit-maximizing behaviour.

Profits over the last year have increased and there are plans for expansion. Ideally the owners would like to reach the status of 'restaurant with rooms'. The computer is the tool which they use to play around with the possibilities: worst case scenarios, having to pay housekeeping staff, that kind of thing. The owners would like to be part of a global reservation system. They feel that there is a big potential in American tourists seeking the 'old world feel' in a small establishment, and this business would not be so seasonal as the current clientele. They feel that American tourist business is sucked into the large anonymous establishments, more because of their computer links tied to airline ticket sales, than consumer choice, and they are actively seeking ways to enter these systems.

Overall their PC has become an integral part of the business, and in terms of proportion of their time spent at the computer, they are more computerized than the most modern, large, chain hotel.

SUMMARY

Throughout the hospitality industry, owners and managers are shaping their own businesses. Sometimes their efforts can be irrelevant to levels of profit. The popularity of an establishment is not just an equation combining product mix, quality of service, value for money and location. Fashions and tastes change and chance should not be ruled out. In the battle of the hospitality entrepreneur against fate (that is, customer demand) his or her skills and techniques are like weapons that they can use in a variety of different ways. Information technology is just one of these weapons, and certainly not the most important one. But in the drive for a successful, profit-maximizing establishment, it is becoming increasingly important.

DISCUSSION TOPICS

To what extent is Wagamama using IT to automate the customer as opposed to informing the manager?

Should 'final destination food stations' have less interest in information technology than 'non-destination food stations'?

If a restaurant is successful, while refusing to use computers, why should it change?

If Forte is the largest hospitality company in Britain, can its corporate culture, the most successful formula, be justified by its success?

Do the motivations of the type of person who sets up his or her own restaurant necessarily mean that they are less interested in profit maximization than other entrepreneurs?

9

The Future: Cyberpunk and the Corporate Computer System

Where I was brought up there was a group of especially tall pines. They had been planted over a century ago, by a sea captain who had seen these pines as a source of masts for future generations of large, wooden, sailships. He had known that they would only be large enough long after he was dead, but had still taken the trouble not just to plant them, but to carry the seeds for a considerable distance.

Inside everyone there is a vision of the future. Sometimes it is explicit, like this chapter and those pine trees. Sometimes it is part of the subconscious, and not even acknowledged; but there is no escape from ideas about what the future will be. The only problem with our concepts of the future is that they are all wrong. While our vision takes a hand in shaping this future, what emerges is something totally different from the sum of individual visions.

Look at how people in the developed world perceived the future in the 1950s. It was a confident vision: modernist architecture, space travel, the end of disease, the end of ideology, characterized above all by a touching faith in the power of technology to improve things. What touches me most about the 1950s' vision is how *clean* the future was going to be.

Our own times have a different vision of the future. Isolated, alienated individuals, crime, environmental crisis, violence, above all the destructive effects of technology: man-made machines stalk the rubble of the future, blowing away human survivors. Yet, within 40 years the populist films of our time will become the amusing curiosities of a future generation of cynical schoolkids (or let's hope so ...). A computerized security system can be marketed on a horror story of a guest who was locked out of her hotel late at night and subsequently raped. The investment in security was not justified in terms of the rape itself, but in the subsequent lawsuit and huge damages for negligence awarded against the hotel, to the guest.

In this chapter we will add to these collections of images of the future, at least in regard to information technology in the hospitality industry, not in any belief that this will be a perfectly accurate picture but to add to discussions about the direction of the hospitality industry. The validity of any theoretical work can be tested by the degree of accuracy of its predictions.

We have already seen that the motivating vision of information technology for the hospitality industry is based on McDonalds. This is technology as an instrument of strong centralized control. Information is measurement to be used for the purposes of evaluation by groups higher up the hierarchy. The aim of technology is predictability, where the behaviour of individual units can be reduced to a set of listed factors. These factors then have an associated list of corrective measures which are to be taken by the upper echelons.

Operatives become units of labour with automated actions and responses, tasks become 'time management units' of almost four-hundredths of a second (Schill and Norback, 1982), ingredients are processed in factories to be reheated or rehydrated on site, supply becomes a worldwide logistical operation with the sophistication of D-Day, customers become units on a conveyor belt, which need certain actions performed on them before they move on down the trough. After a fashion, the whole process does work. McDonalds is still profitable and expanding, they do listen to the suggestions of their staff, customers queue and are refuelled; they generally leave without complaining. That 1950s' vision of technology lives on in McDonalds, not least in the fanatical cleanliness.

The hospitality industry is still caught up in this paradigm. Information systems are designed where the primary function is to provide units of measure, which will enable the centre to evaluate, compare and discipline local units. League tables are automatically compiled and distributed, reports are demanded the same day, problems and blame are sought and distributed. Of course, these activities were always inherent in companies, but the management information systems are designed with these activities in mind. They speed up the process. Monitoring, evaluation and control takes on a whole new dimension when information is so quickly available.

To some extent this paradigm does not work. All too easily it can become a 'high-cost, no-delivery system, locked in an ivory tower' (First Leisure IT executive). We have seen the group of managers who evaluate success as the perceptions of their seniors. This tendency in managers is enhanced by the use of information technology systems. In the same way that IT will not stop bar fiddles, management information systems do not stop management putting a good light on their actions. These systems just mean that managers have to be more sophisticated in how they choose to present information.

The more rigid and structured the system, the less flexibility and creativity local management has in responding to fresh problems and local conditions. A company can overcome this with such a strongly branded product and image, that the last thing they want from their management is creativity and flexibility. When breakfast *burritos* are the upper end of the company's creativity spectrum, this can be quite safely handled by the centre. However, most companies need a flexible and responsive management corps.

Small companies too are infected by the McDonalds paradigm. In their search for autonomy and a certain quality of life, the owner-manager rejects the inflexibility of the McDonalds use of computers. It simply does not fit their idea of what they want from their business, and the way in which it should be done. There is irony in the fact that in other industries, this could be precisely the sector which would make most beneficial use of the new technology.

NEW WAYS

Throughout the text we have seen possibilities that information technology opens up. The McDonalds image is simply the industrial revolution at a new level of machine sophistication. However, in three distinct areas we have seen the potential for change in the hospitality industry: product or service, the organization itself and the way in which people work.

New Services

Looking at the product or service itself, most theories about product development are taken from the manufacturing industry. Classical product life cycle theory (e.g. Kuznets, 1953) suggests that there is an introductory phase with a major product innovation. This has a diversity of new products and is very labour-intensive. Gradually, though, the introduction phase is replaced by a growth phase, which is characterized by increasing capital intensity, and lower unit costs of production. The variety of product innovations are gradually reduced as one form increasingly dominates. For example, the initially wide variety of video recorders is replaced almost by one type, which has a much reduced cost. For McDonalds too, restaurants have become more capital-intensive, the variety of hamburgers they sell has diminished and unit costs have declined in real terms. However it would be difficult to claim the overall hamburger product had become less differentiated.

Barras (1986) has criticized the application of the product cycle theory to the transformations that new technology is bringing to the service sector. He has developed his own 'reverse product theory' which stresses the unique characteristics of the service sector, and the unique changes that information technology is bringing about.

His first stage is the application of information technology 'designed to increase the efficiency of delivery of existing services'. This is the stage which we are in at the moment, with the emphasis placed on reductions in cost. The second stage is the technology being applied to 'improving the quality of the services'. This type of approach is only found in isolated pockets in the hospitality industry. The final stage is when the technology 'assists in generating wholly transformed or new services'.

In traditional product theory the variety of products is reduced as the innovation works its way through an industry. In Barras's reverse product cycle the variety of products/services is increased as the innovation matures within an industry. Barras's research was concentrated on the financial services sector, but it has applications for the hospitality industry. He noted that in the early stages 'the first phase of technical progress in services tends to have a strong labour saving bias'. And this is certainly something we have seen in the hotel and catering industry.

As an illustration of the reverse product theory remote order pads represent an attempt to increase efficiency, as more customers are processed, and the food server does not have to deliver the order to the kitchen. Food and beverage control systems are developed with the intention of reducing costs, by cutting back on pilfering or wastage. Reservation systems enable operatives to process more customers. These are all examples of attempts to use information technology to reduce costs. Motivating this is the (usually thwarted) management desire to reduce staffing levels.

Stage two of Barras's theory could simply be a more detailed bill, the provision of nutritional information, a menu tailored to the preferences of the customer, or the previous details of a guest's stay used by the receptionist: 'Would you like your old room?' The same technology could be used in different ways. Remote order pads could enable the waiter to spend more time chatting with the customer, as opposed to simply processing more customers. The reservations operative could use technology to provide a choice to the customer, fitting the specific needs of the client. All of these are improvements in quality.

The final stage of the generation of new services has hardly begun, and as Barras admitted, technically we are not talking about new services. Provision of food and lodging are the services, and these do not really change. What changes is the modes of delivery, and these change so radically that they can appear like new services. Pizza home delivery services owe part of their growth to computerized systems. As information becomes increasingly computerized, establishments can tailor their products, more and more for the niche markets. At the moment a hotel can specialize in the gay market, or be women-only. What if a hotel specialized in vegan teenagers, who booked the hotel at an hourly rate? A frivolous example, but it would certainly be a different type of hotel. In fact, to have any chance of success, it could not call itself a hotel.

Barras noted three consequences of the reverse product cycle. First, the locus of delivery shifts from the point of production to the point of consumption: the meal and lodging is resited more where the consumer is, as opposed to where the restaurant and hotel used to be. The modern fashion to put the kitchen on show to dining customers, or even to cook directly in front of the customer is connected to this. Second, there is an increasing emphasis on flexibility and better information for the consumer. Finally, producer-consumer relationships change as knowledge is computerized.

Chapter 2 explored the interaction between the consumer and information technology. This combination of new consumer attitudes and the potential of advanced technology will ensure that the way in which hospitality services are provided changes dramatically. There will always be a place for an unworldly retreat from the modern world: but it will increasingly be equipped with an information system that enables the establishment to preserve its façade.

New Organizations

Large hospitality organizations are a classic example of how an organization can use information technology ineffectively. Cumbersomely bureaucratic, inflexibly hierarchical forms are inappropriate when it comes to generating new services and responding to a fickle clientele. It is possible that they may suit a large, well-established company, acting as a 'defender' of its position, but technological change means new organizational forms.

Modern writers on business organization favour 'dynamic networks' (Miles and Snow, 1986, p.165) of constantly changing groups of people: 'Ways of doing business traditionally have been highly contingent on ways of organizing, and major competitive breakthroughs have been achieved by firms that invented, or were quick to apply, new forms of organization and management.' This we have not yet seen in the hospitality industry. The success of some of the newly established large independent restaurants (e.g. Wagamama) is the closest we have come to this so far.

The new organizational forms will have a number of distinct features. First, they will be characterized by vertical disintegration. Complicated divisional structures, with extended hierarchies, will not disappear, but they will be eroded and threatened by more collective enterprises. These collective enterprises (e.g. a small group of hotels, a chain of restaurants) will need to come together for specific projects. Perhaps they need to work together to maximize the bargaining power with a strong supplier, perhaps they need to come to an arrangement about sharing resources such as marketing expertise. To foster these temporary alliances of self-interest there will need to be a series of brokers. These are people or organizations that can bring companies together and negotiate mutually beneficial solutions.

The collective enterprises could correspond to the old divisions of a hospitality corporation. Without the same hierarchical structure, how is the collective enterprise to be motivated? In the past, a traditional inducement might be the movement of an individual up the corporate hierarchy. This type of inducement will be replaced by an increasing reliance on market mechanisms as a means of enforcement. If a collective enterprise does badly, it is replaced. If it does well it is handsomely rewarded. This will tie in with new ways of working, which we will turn to later.

Another characteristic of the new-style hospitality organization will be full-disclosure information systems. The process of temporary alliances and co-operation will be cemented with computer systems which make everything available to all parts of the pact. The information systems will be like the glue for what could be very disparate companies.

Restaurant franchises in hotels are not a new concept. However, suppose the room-service food ordering system linked to the guest's TV provided the facilities of local restaurants, as well as the cling-filmed abominations which make up the usual fare. Both organizations could potentially benefit from this type of arrangement, but to demonstrate this, they would both need full access to information on the system.

Responsiveness to change will be the fundamental determinant of the new hospitality organization. 'The dynamic network is a far more flexible structure than any of the previous forms, it can accommodate a vast amount of complexity while maximising specialised competence' (Miles and Snow, 1986, p.64).

New Ways of Working

Chapter 3 showed the new informating force of information technology. Essentially, information that was previously the province of management comes within the grasp of the operative. Operatives have more control over their work, are becoming more skilled, need less supervision and have more responsibility. This is an inexorable trend which is as yet unremarked and unutilized by the hospitality industry.

A receptionist has available a large amount of information. When the guest walks in and presents the receptionist with a problem, the traditional response might be to involve line management. Neither the guest nor the receptionist necessarily seeks this. With more information available to the receptionist, the problem can be solved: the guest resited, a query answered, a rate confirmed. It is increasingly possible for the receptionist to provide a solution for the problem, as opposed to simply flagging it for management.

The reservations operative is crucial to the maximizing of the hotel's room revenue. It is claimed that the first six words can make or break a potential sale. All too often these can be 'let me just check for you'. With information about targets, expected levels of occupancy, rates, and current levels (and type) of bookings the operative is more likely to take a decision which will beneficially impact on room revenue.

The waiter too has more information available. The hand-held device can inform the waiter when an ordered item has just run out. Orders can be managed with suggested replacements, all without recourse to nipping into the kitchen for a quick check with the chefs. Perhaps the waiter can manage bookings and tables to ensure a more even flow of work. It might be possible to utilize the selling techniques of the waiter to maximize revenue, by pushing the more profitable items. Information can be provided for the waiter and used for incentive purposes.

At every level the nature of work is changing. It is more marked in other industries, but even there it is just the beginning of a process. If you had responsibility for a large computerized hotel, how might you change room rates? Pricing is one of the most crucial decisions for any business and the aim is to maximize your profits: too high you drive business away, too low and you fail to cover your costs.

Of course, as is often the case, the decision could be taken for you by head office. Second, the senior management team could gather together and take the decision after a discussion. It is unlikely that outside help has been called in, and within this team there are different approaches and emphases. Perhaps the food and beverage manager, or the conference and banqueting manager favour a lower rate? Eventually, after a discussion, the decision is taken by the general manager.

A third option might be to involve the reservations operatives and their line management. They might be the most aware group on the effect of pricing changes. They have detailed data on the effect of pricing changes in the past, they have the most precise sense of what motivates client decisions and they have specific information on trends.

If the reservations team were responsible for the decision, what would be the best way of taking the decision? There would be a general discussion, when operatives would throw up suggestions and ideas. With computers available to the team, this would lead to the testing of these ideas on the system. Data would be examined to discover previous patterns, future strategies could be costed on the basis of existing information.

The absence of strong divisions between authority levels would foster open suggestion of ideas and hypotheses testing which were not related to positions in the hotel hierarchy. Motivation could be ensured by tying group remuneration to levels of improvement in room revenues. The access of information fosters an almost collegial style of decision-making, where the emphasis is on contribution and team, rather than directives and levels of authority. Quite often the senior management team, through their reports and briefing documents, are trying to achieve the same level of knowledge as their operatives.

Of course there is no large hotel where any team of operatives has any significant input into the setting of price points. So removed is this from conventional reality in the hospitality industry, that it has all the hallmarks of heresy. Part of the heresy is that operatives might not welcome that degree of responsibility, certainly not on the wages that they are currently receiving. The irony is that they are groups of operatives who do use their increased access to information to experiment with ideas, admittedly these ideas are ignored in their vacuum, but there are people who work in reservations who have sophisticated ideas about pricing that seem to be improvements.

The main reason why the informating force of the new technology is not acknowledged in the hospitality industry is the role of management. As Tom Peters wrote (quoted in Bowen and Lawler, 1992, p.32): 'It is impossible to get people's best efforts, involvement, and caring concern for things you believe important to your customers and the long term interests of your organization when we write policies and procedures that treat them like thieves and bandits.' Or in the words of an interviewed operative: 'Managers perceive workers who have information as a threat.'

Chapter 5 commented on a group which has a sense of identity and self-interest which can sometimes transcend their role of profit maximizers. Hospitality management defines its *raison d'être* as control. Control of operations, control of operatives and control of the information systems which they put in place. Bailey (1993, p.111) talks of the 'managerial tabernacle', where managers see themselves as the repository of the highest knowledge and skills: 'the truth'.

When the revolutionary implications of information technology were first realized, it was thought that middle management would be eroded by the new technology, as their controlling function was replaced by machines. It is clear that this is no longer the case: middle management is practically a growth industry in itself. However, if the industry is going to move to a more fruitful application of the benefits of information technology, the role of the manager has to change.

No longer is he or she the controller of information which is distributed by the will of the manager. Whether they like it or not, the information has moved on from just the manager. Increasingly the manager will have exactly the same access to information as the operative. The first consequence will be a blurring of the distinction between manager and operative. As the title of manager has such status, one consequence might be the increasing sight of teams of people all terming themselves managers.

The second consequence will be the increasing use of teams in the hospitality industry. Not in the sense of the mock 'teams' found in the fast-food industry, but in the sense of work groups formed around a common purpose and associated information system, rather than a grade of hierarchy. This will have significant implications for levels of remuneration, and job security.

Motivation and discipline will, as for the 'virtual corporations' discussed above, come through the market. If the team performs to target, then it is well rewarded. If it does not achieve target, then the group runs the risk of being replaced. Patterns of work are changing, and there is an increasing shift towards a disrupted pattern, based on vacillations in the market and the ability to respond. Skills in information processing will become paramount, associated with a renewed emphasis on creative problem-solving and imagination – not skills traditionally associated with hospitality management.

Although these skills will be IT-based, this does not mean that they will consist of a manager locked in a room with a computer. The intuitive reasoning of an old-style hospitality manager is not replaced by a barren, statistics-driven approach. The computer assists in the work, rather than dominates it. As an interviewed IT manager put it: 'We need to teach the business revenues people the old skills, like looking at the weather.' How is any computer going to deal with the impact of variables like the Lockerbie air disaster, rail strikes and salmonella scares? In these situations the computer assists the manager plan responses; it does not predict customer responses.

The hospitality manager him or herself will have to demonstrate a new style of management. Instead of emphasizing control through information transfer, the new emphasis will be on leadership: the same skills of creativity and flexibility, but more so. The manager manages by breaking down barriers, creating the atmosphere that will enable him or her to 'get people's best efforts'. An important part of that role will be one of teacher: providing the operative with the confidence and skill to experiment with the system, try out new approaches, and relate these to business targets. 'Managers should be drivers of learning' (Zuboff, 1988, p.280).

It is possible that the successful hospitality manager will even look different, as the prejudices of the selectors move away from tall, white, males. One possible reason for the prejudices in favour of this type is its association with a more 'forceful' style of management.

New concepts of management are not currently part of the hospitality industry. Only once have I found a consciousness of the dramatic consequences of IT on management: 'You can't just replace what we had before with a computer and keep the same management structures' (Information systems director for Scott Marriott). At the moment a hotel front office manager might have a series of people working underneath him or her: porters, telephonists, receptionists, guest relations people and perhaps reservations people. This would be represented graphically as a hierarchical tree.

The interviewed IT director drew a possible new structure as three interlocking circles of business, guest services and process. The business function would involve the managing and maximizing of revenue and would include salespeople. Guest services would be ensuring the happiness of guests: delivering the room at the right price and time. Process would involve the supervision and maintenance of the computer system to ensure the first two sections could do their job. Integral to the new vision was the impact of information technology in changing the way in which work was carried out. The whole structure would be much flatter, with, in effect, the general manager co-ordinating a series of teams. 'Management becomes much more of a "process" in which everyone can participate, rather than the prerogative of the privileged few' (Bailey, 1993, p.183).

One odd problem of this type of structure is the issue of progression or promotion. At present, if superiors are positive about staff performance, they can be moved into the next level, working their way up the hierarchy step by step until they reach their level of incompetence. However, a flatter structure works against this type of incremental progression. Career patterns in the future are much more likely to be an uneven set of hops and jumps, as people improve their income through more dramatic changes.

Information technology will change the way in which work is carried out. There will be increasing autonomy for local units, even if they reside in a loose, corporate structure. Certain large, Jewish restaurants have a traditional way of working that makes the waiters self-employed. The food and drink is sold, at a discount, to the waiter, who then sells it on to the customer. Service charge, cash handling and customer relations all become the waiter's business. In effect it makes the operative a partner in the enterprise. One consequence of this is an unusual style of service, not so servile, more entertainingly rude.

This is an uncommon way of working, partly because of the administrative workload for the restaurant in selling food to the food serving staff. However, this is one method of operation which could be very easily handled by a food and beverage management system. The style of operation makes the restaurant an explicit co-operation between restaurant and (some) operatives: the waiters have a vested interest in the restaurant.

Apart from potentially more autonomous individuals, and work teams, local units themselves could become more autonomous. 'Operational flexibility' currently built into budgets could be extended, so that the establishment was set very broad financial targets. What local management teams and operatives did to achieve those targets would be their own responsibility. One consequence might be the erosion of some strongly branded products. If the establishment wished to be part of the brand for their own advantage, they would. However, some would decide the advantage to the establishment lay outside the brand.

In London, probably the highest concentration of eating establishments is around the Soho area. The clientele is an affluent, fashion-conscious and well-informed section of the market. It is interesting that chain restaurants have failed to make any significant impact on the area. A number have tried and most have failed. The customers are looking for a unique product and service. Perhaps chain restaurants are going to be increasingly filled by customers who are there because of TV advertising directed at their children.

THE STRUGGLE CONTINUES

A number of writers in this area make the assertion that the informating effect of the new technology will have an inexorable force, sweeping us into some kind of anarcho-syndicalist Utopia. Yet all that this book has outlined is the battlefield that surrounds the application of information technology in the hospitality industry.

On one side we have the traditionally autocratic hospitality corporation, which uses computers for control and calculability. On the other side we have the creative, informating side of information technology, which grows with every little experiment on the microcomputer. 'Informating typically unfolds as an objective un-planned autonomous process' (Zuboff, 1988, p.306). The two sides are on a collision course, but it would be wrong to assume that either one could triumph totally.

Part of the resistance to the informating process will be the way the manager refuses to adapt. We have seen how hospitality managers will be resistant to the undermining of authority, of their power and their differentiation from the operative. Educational establishments are producing a managerial caste that is even more conscious of its own distinct identity than the managers of a previous generation. The latter group largely consisted of craft-level operatives who had been promoted. The younger group has a sense of identity earned by years in college (and student loans). It sees itself as a meritocracy, and it is not necessarily less resistant to an information strategy which 'undermines' its position, even when it perceives itself as less technophobic.

More important than the manager will be the behaviour of the customer. There is a gradual shift towards providing the customer with tender loving care. However, when companies such as Taco Bell can believe that their production line approach gives them the competitive edge, the informating shift is hardly inexorable. Taco Bell's argument is that the customer does not want any meaningful relationship with the person who gives them the food. What the Taco Bell consumer wants (argues Taco Bell) is a cheap product delivered as quickly as possible. How would you feel about a friendly food server, when he or she is being friendly to the person in front of you in the queue?

Tender loving care, or flexibility, has to be paid for, and the crucial determinant is how much the consumer is willing to pay. I have heard it suggested, by a hospitality manager, that the main reason why the business customer wants a more personal service is that he or she is generally not paying with their own money.

The flexible, imaginative use of computers will probably be introduced through the agency of those on the fringes of the hospitality industry, e.g. consultants. Freelance consultants will be increasingly pulled in by companies in an attempt to give creativity and flair to an organization which does not support IT itself: creative destroyers. In effect, consultants are the decriminalized deviants who can be used to break the rules and codes of an organization – rather like the hackers who become consultants on computer security. The consultant will chat to some operatives and say 'why don't you do it this way', and for the next few years operatives will be doing it precisely that way. But these operatives will not know why they are doing it that way, and they might have had a better suggestion in the first place.

This underlines the fundamental power of operatives with access to an information system. Nothing can underscore more the potential of an informated operator than an automated worker: a worker who does precisely what he or she is told. A worker who ignores possible improvements to an operation, or who has his or her suggestions ignored is a waste. It is a waste for the consumer, a waste for the company and a waste for the operative: 'Let's do something different today.'

> *'Using the technology to its full potential, means using the man to his full potential.'*
>
> *(Zuboff, 1988, p.414.)*

DISCUSSION TOPICS

Does McDonalds better suit the 1950s than the twenty-first century?

What new modes of service delivery could information technology open up in the provision of food and lodging?

In a world of unceasing change, do some consumers find the certainty of an unchanging product or service reassuring?

With an egalitarian organizational structure, do we need general managers, and, if we do, how do we find them?

Is a university-generated cadre of hospitality managers a hindrance or an asset to an informated approach to information systems development?

Is information technology education for future hospitality managers ghettoized?

GLOSSARY

Computers seem to breed acronyms, in fact they seem a compulsory feature of any discussion of information technology. In the text of this book I have deliberately tried to avoid using them. The use of acronyms should not be confused with knowledge, but here are a few either to use yourself or to help decipher conversations.

AI Artificial Intelligence
Programming a computer so that it can think in a human manner. This involves developing a set of rules which the computer uses to attempt to solve problems.
BEO Banquet Event Order
Consolidation of information on a banquet, with information taken from the function book. The BEO usually becomes the final contract for the client.
CAD Computer-Aided Design
CDU Customer Display Unit
A screen, usually sited on top of the POS, which gives the customer information on purchases.
CPU Central Processing Unit
Slightly dated term for the control centre of a computer, as distinct from the monitor, printer etc.
CRO Central Reservations Office

A computer reservations system for a chain of hotels, accessed by the public, usually with an easy-to-remember telephone number. It acts as a clearing house for reservations with these hotels.

DMS Database Management System

Software that stores, organizes and retrieves data in a database.

DSS Decision Support System

Increasingly important aspect of information technology aiming to support decision-makers. Quite often focused on just one aspect of the business.

ECR Electronic Cash Register

Normally considered to be a standalone point of sales device. With its own memory and processing capacity it is a computer in its own right.

EDI Electronic Data Interchange

Computers communicating with other computers, usually through telephone lines. It could be used to pay the wages of staff or send an order to a supplier.

EFT Electronic Funds Transfer

Money 'changing hands' through the medium of a computer.

EFTPOS Electronic Funds Transfer at the Point of Sales

As above but carried out in (for example) the restaurant or hotel.

EPOS Electronic Point of Sale

An EPOS terminal is a till linked to a central computer which can analyse the data from several terminals.

GDS Global Distribution System

An international system linking the consumer, usually via travel agents, to future purchases such as airline tickets, hotels and car hire. Examples of these systems in the UK would include Gallileo and Sabre.

HIS Hotel Information System

I/O Input/Output

A connection or 'port' through which the computer communicates with external devices e.g. a printer.

IT Information Technology

KB Kilobyte

Unit of memory for a computer, used for purposes of comparison. It consists of 1,024 Bytes.

LAN Local Area Network

Computers linked up in such a way that they can share output devices (usually printers), data or programs. Usually restricted in scale, for example to a floor of a building.

MB Megabyte

Another unit of computer memory, consisting of 1,048,576 bytes.

MHz Megahertz

This is used to measure and compare the processing speed of a computer.

MIS Management Information System

Allegedly a system to provide management with information necessary to do its job.

MSDOS Microsoft Disk Operating System
A disk operating system orchestrates the hardware which you are using, without it none of your programs would work. Microsoft is a company which provides the most common DOS for the PC market.
OCk Optical Character Recognition
Increasingly important way in which the computer can recognize and store typed documentation.
PC Personal Computer
A type of microcomputer, originally developed by IBM, which is still dominant in the business world.
PLU Price Look-Up
A code on a POS which identifies a menu item. The PLU can be used when entering an order or in subsequent analysis.
PMS Property Management System
An integrated computer system used throughout a hotel.
POS Point of Sale
RAM Random Access Memory
That part of the computer's memory which is lost when you switch it off.
REPOS Remote Entry Point of Sales Device
A hand-held electronic order pad.
RMS Restaurant Management System
ROM Read Only Memory
The part of the computer's memory which is not lost when the computer is switched off.
RTC Real Time Clock
A hardware device that ensures date and time is accurate despite power failures.
RTFM Read the *** manual**
Oft quoted basic advice.
SCMS Sales and Conference Management System
SEP Somebody Else's Problem
SQL Structured Query Language
A language that is becoming a standard for retrieving data from databases.
TLC Tender Loving Care
A service enrichment strategy.
UNIX
An operating system for 16-bit computers.
VDU Visual Display Unit
The television screen (usually) on top of the computer which displays video information stored in the computer. Also called a monitor.
VRS Voice Recognition Systems
Developing technology which enables computers to respond to verbal instructions.

BIBLIOGRAPHY

Aspden, P. (1994) 'Carp pool reflections on the art of doubt', *The Times Higher*, 22 April.

Bailey, J. (1993) *Managing People and Technological Change*, Pitman Publishing, London.

Barras, R. (1986) 'Towards a theory of innovation in services', *Research Policy*, Vol. 15, Part 5, pp. 161–73.

Barras, R. (1990) 'Interactive innovation in financial and business services: The vanguard of the service revolution', *Research Policy* Vol. 19, Part 5, pp. 215–37.

Bilkey, M. A. and Norback, J. P. (1986) 'Using common ingredient units', *Journal of Food Service Systems*, Vol. 4, Part 1, pp. 47-58.

Blackman, D. (1989) 'Automation survey', *Hotel Management Today*, 10 November.

Blackwell, R. (1992) 'Out of the frying pan: A study of stress in the hospitality industry', *Leeds Polytechnic Discussion Papers in Hospitality Management*, Leeds.

Boer, A. (1992) 'The banking sector and small firm failure in the UK hotel and catering industry', *International Journal of Contemporary Hospitality Management*, Vol. 4, No. 2, pp. 13–16.

Bosworth, D. L. (ed.) (1983) *The Employment Consequences of Technological Change*, Nottingham, Skills and Enterprise Network.

Bowen, D. E. and Lawler III, E. E. (1992) 'The empowerment of service workers: What, why, how and when', *Sloan Management Review*, Spring, pp. 31–9.

Boyce, A. F. (1985) 'Just like the electronic home', *Communications*, May, pp. 19–21.

Boyce, A. F. (1991) 'Maximise yields', *Caterer and Hotelkeeper*, 24 January.

Bozymski, M. (1985) 'The crucial link', *Restaurant Business*, 20 March, pp. 151–2.

Braham, B. (1988) *Computer Systems in the Hotel and Catering Industry*, Cassell, London.

Brotherton, R. and Leslie, D. (1991) 'Critical information needs for achieving strategic goals', in R. Teare and A. Boer (eds.) *Strategic Hospitality Management*, Cassell, London, pp. 33–44.

Brownell, J. (1992) 'Hospitality managers' communication practices', *International Journal of Hospitality Management*, Vol. 11, No. 2, pp. 111–28.

Buchanan, D. A. and McCalman J. (1988) 'Confidence, visibility and pressure: The effects of shared information in computer aided hotel management', *New Technology, Work & Employment*, pp. 38–46.

Burrows, R. (1991) 'The discourse of the enterprise culture and the restructuring of Britain – A polemical contribution', in J. Curran and R. A. Blackburn, (eds) *Paths of Enterprise*, Routledge, London pp. 17–33.

Chia, R. (1992) *Modern and Postmodern Thinking Styles: Implications for Organizational Analysis*, unpublished paper, October.

Clark, P. and Staunton, N. (1989) *Innovation in Technology and Organisation*, Routledge, London.

Cooper, C. and Buhalis, D. (1992) 'Strategic management and marketing of small and medium-sized tourism enterprises in the Greek Aegean', *Managing Projects in Hospitality Organisations*, Cassell, London, pp. 101–24.

Craver, D. (1990) 'Training the hybrids in their own image', *Computer Weekly*, 5 April, p. 16.

Crawford-Welch, S. (1993a) 'Competitive marketing strategies in the international hospitality industry', in R. Teare (ed.) *International Hospitality Management*, Pitman Publishing, London.

Crawford-Welch, S. (1993b) 'The international hospitality consumer', in P. Jones and A. Pizam (eds) *The International Hospitality Industry*, Pitman Publishing, London, pp. 189–204.

Curran, J. and Blackburn, R. (1991a) 'Changes in the context of enterprise – some socio-economic and environmental factors facing small firms in the 1990s', *Paths of Enterprise*, Routledge, London, pp. 163–92.

Curran, J. and Blackburn, R. A. (eds) (1991b) *Paths of Enterprise*, Routledge, London.

Curran, J., Blackburn R. A. and Jarvis R. (1990) *Small Firms and Local Networks: Some Theoretical and Conceptual Explorations*

Daniel, W. W. (1987) *Workplace Industrial Relations and Technical Change*, Frances Pinter, Shaftesbury.

Dickson, K., Smith, S. L. and Woods, A. (1991a) *Innovation and Co-operation in Small Service Sector Enterprises*, unpublished paper.

Dickson, K., Smith, S. L., Louise, R. and Woods, A. (1991b) *Technological Innovation and Small Service Sector Enterprises*, paper to 14th National Small Firms Conference, Blackpool.

Dronfield, L. and Soto, P. (1981) *Hardship Hotel* London, Counter Information Services.

Eddystone, C., Braunlich, C. G. and Zhang, Y. (1994) 'Career paths in American luxury hotels: Hotel food and beverage directors', *International Journal of Contemporary Hospitality Management*, Vol. 6, No. 6, pp. 3–9.

Finley, P.N., Forsey, G. and Holland, P. (1987) 'The small hotelier and the banker: A computerised system to satisfy the common information needs', *The Services Industry Journal*, Vol. 6, No. 2, pp. 308–18.

Forrest, J. E. (1991) 'Models of the process of technological innovation', *Technology Analysis and Strategic Management*, Vol. 3, No. 4, pp. 439–53.

Gamble, P. R. (1984) *Small computers and hospitality management*, London, Hutchinson Education.

Gamble, P. R. (1987) 'Hotech 87', *International Journal of Hospitality Management*, Vol. 6, No. 4, pp. 250–1.

Gamble, P. R. (1988a) 'Attitudes to computers by managers in the hospitality industry', *Behaviour and Information Technology*, Vol. 7, No. 3, pp. 305–21.

Gamble, P. R. (1988b) 'Tourism technology: Developing effective computer systems', *Tourism Management*, Vol. 9, No. 4, pp. 317–25.

Gamble, P. R. (1990) 'Developing an information technology strategy for hospitality organisations', *International Journal of Contemporary Hospitality Management*, Vol. 1, pp. 29–41.

Gamble, P. R. (1991a) 'An information technology strategy for the hospitality industry of the 1990s', *International Journal of Contemporary Hospitality Management*, Vol. 3, No. 1, pp. 10–15.

Gamble, P. R. (1991b) 'Inaugural lecture – innovation and innkeeping', *International Journal of Hospitality Management*, Vol. 10, No. 1, pp. 3–23.

Gamble, P. R. (1993) 'The strategic role of information technology systems', in R. Teare (ed.) *International Hospitality Management*, Pitman Publishing, London.

Gamble, P. R. and Jones, P. (1991) 'Quality as a strategic issue', in R. Teare and A. Boer (eds.) *Strategic Hospitality Management*, Cassell, London, pp. 72–82.

Gamble, P. R. and Mitchell I. D. (1987) 'Editorial', *International Journal of Hospitality Management*, Vol. 6, No. 4, p. 189.

Gamble, P. R. and Smith G. (1986) 'Expert front office management by computer', *International Journal of Hospitality Management*, Vol. 5, No. 3, pp. 109–14.

Gindin, R. L. (1984) 'Computers in foodservice', *Restaurant Business*, 1 July, pp. 83–148.

Glaser, B. G. and Strauss, A. L. (1967) *The Discovery of Grounded Theory*, Aldine de Gruyter, New York.

Goymour, D. (1989) 'Solutions for sale', *Hotech '89 Catalogue*, October, pp. 20–1.

Harris, K. J. (1994) 'Multimedia: fluff, fashion or future?', *International Journal of Hospitality Management*, Vol. 12, No. 4, pp. 367–84.

Hankinson, A., (1989) 'Small hotels in Britain: Investment and survival', *Cornell HRA Quarterly*, November, pp. 80–2.

HCITB (1981) *Choosing a Microcomputer*, February.

Hermanson, E. D. (1979) 'Analysis of food decision making strategies', *Dissertation Abstracts International*, B 1980 40, Part 11, 5209.

Johnson, K. (1980) 'Staff turnover in hotels', *Hospitality*, February, pp. 28–36.

Johnson, K. (1983) 'Trade unions and total rewards', *International Journal of Hospitality Management*, Vol. 2, No. 1, pp. 31–5.

Johns, N. and Wheeler, K. (1991) 'Productivity and performance measurement and monitoring', in R. Teare and A. Boer (eds.) *Strategic Hospitality Management*, Cassell, London, pp. 45–71.

Jones, P. A. and Norton, J. (1992) 'Implementing a catering information system in the armed forces (Army Catering Corps)', *Managing Projects in Hospitality Organisations*, Cassell, London, pp. 129–45.

Jones, P. L. and Goss-Turner, S. (1992) 'Creativity for hospitality managers (Forte plc)', *Managing Projects in Hospitality Organisations*, Cassell, London, pp. 311–25.

Kasavana, M. L. (1987) 'Hotel multiprocessor environments: Guest and non-guest operated interfaces', *International Journal of Hospitality Management*, Vol. 6, No. 4, pp. 217–24.

Kasavana, M. L. and Cahill J. J. (1987) *Managing Computers in the Hospitality Industry*, Educational Institute, East Lansing.

Keegan, J. (1993) *A History of Warfare*, Hutchinson, London.

Kimes, S. E. (1994) 'Perceived fairness of yield management', *Cornell HRA Quarterly*, February, pp. 22–9.

Kuznets, S. (1953) *Economic Change*, Norton, New York.

Mankinson, A. (1989) 'Small hotels in Britain: Investment and survival', *Cornell HRA Quarterly*, November, pp. 80–2.

Marinko, B. A. (1990) 'POS for the 1990s addresses flexibility', *Hotel and Motel Management*, 10 September, pp. 85–8.

Mars, G. (1982), revd 1994, *Cheats at Work: An Anthropology of Workplace Crime*, Dartmouth, Aldershot.

Matthews, M. E. (1983) 'Foodservice information framework', *Food Technology*, Vol. 37, Part 12, pp. 46–54.

McCool, A. C. (1986) 'Computer technology in institutional foodservice', *Journal of American Dietetic Association*, Vol. 86, No. 1, January, pp. 48–56.

McCool, A. C. (1987) 'Some considerations in developing expert systems for the hospitality industry', *International Journal of Hospitality Management*, Vol. 6, No. 4, pp. 191–8.

McLouglin, I. and Clark, J. (1988) *Technological Change at Work*, Open University Press, Buckingham.

McMahon, R. G. P. (1990) 'Expert systems and financial decision support in small businesses', *International Small Business Journal*, Vol. 8, No. 2, pp. 20–33.

Miles, R. E. and Snow, C. C. (1986) 'Organisations: New concepts for new forms', *California Management Review*, Vol. 28, No. 3, Spring, pp. 62–73.

Miller, S. G. (1988) 'Creating menus with desktop publishing', *Cornell HRA Quarterly*, February, pp. 32–5.

Mitchell, I. (1989) 'On-line for business as hoteliers gear up', *Caterer & Hotelkeeper*, 16 February, pp. 77–9.

Mitchell, J. C. (1973) 'Networks, norms & institutions', in J. Boissevain (ed.) *Network Analysis Studies in Human Interaction*, Mouton, The Hague, pp. 15–36.

Murray, R. (1985) Benetton Britain, *Marxism Today*, October.

Nissan, E. (1987a) 'Knowledge-based computer systems for tasks in hospitality management or related areas: Accommodation (lodging alimentation) and leisure', *International Journal of Hospitality Management*, Vol. 6, No. 4, pp. 199–202.

Nissan, E. (1987b) 'The "Wining and Dining" Project', *International Journal of Hospitality Management*, Vol. 6, No. 4, pp. 203–15.

Northcott, J. (1986) *Microelectronics in Industry*, Policy Studies Institute Research Report 657.

Oakey, R., Rothwell, R. and Cooper, S. (1988) *The Management of Innovation in High Technology Small Firms*, Pinter Publishers, London.

Peacock, M. (1993a) 'A question of size', *International Journal of Contemporary Hospitality Management*, Vol. 5, No. 4, pp. 29–32.

Peacock, M. (1993b) 'Towards a new consumer', *International Journal of Hospitality Management*, Vol. 11, No. 4, pp. 301–4.

Peacock, M. (1994a) 'Creativity and information technology, the relationship between hospitality management education and advanced technological change, 'Innovations in Teaching & Learning' Conference, Leeds.

Peacock, M. (1994b) 'Dear Doctor Ludd: Some questions on the hospitality industry and advanced technological change', *International Journal of Hospitality Management*, Vol. 13, No. 1, pp. 19–24.

Peacock, M. (1994c) 'Hospitality managers who love computers too little? An investigation into the relationship between management and advanced technological change', paper for CHME research conference, Edinburgh.

Peacock, M. (1995) ' "A job well done": Hospitality Managers and Success', paper for CHME Research Conference, Norwich.

Peacock, M., Reeve, R. and Shaw, H. (1994) ' "Spend money on that?" Investment appraisal in the hospitality industry', *International Journal of Contemporary Hospitality Management*, Vol. 6, No. 6, pp. i–iii.

Pine, R. (1987) *Management of Technological Change in the Catering Industry*, Avebury, Aldershot.

Pine, R. (1992) 'Technology transfer in the hotel industry', *International Journal of Hospitality Management*, Vol. 11, Part 1, pp. 3–22.

Pine, R. (1993) 'Technology transfer in the hotel industry', in P. Jones and A. Pizam (eds) *The International Hospitality Industry*, Pitman Publishing, London, pp. 226–40.

Pine, R. J. (1985) Catering Technology – Some issues for effective utilisation, M. Phil. thesis, Huddersfield Polytechnic.

Porter, M. E. and Millar, V. E. (1985) 'How information gives you competitive advantage', *Harvard Business Review*, July/August, pp. 149–60.

Pringle, S. M. (1994) *International reservations systems*, Edinburgh, paper for CHME research conference.

Quinn, U., Larmour, R. and McQuillan, N. (1992) 'The small firm in the hospitality industry', *International Journal of Contemporary Hospitality Management*, Vol. 4, No. 1, pp. 11–14.

Raho, L. E. (1986) 'Strategic thinking and the PC: Some policy considerations', *Journal of Information Systems Management*, Autumn, pp. 52–7.

Reeve, R. (1994) *The Impact of IT on the Modern Hotel*, London, unpublished paper.

Reid, R. (1986) *Land of Lost Content, The Luddite Revolt, 1812*, Heinemann, London.

Ritzer, G. (1993) *The McDonaldization of Society*, Pine Forge Press, Newbury Park, California.

Rothwell, R. (1977) 'Characteristics of successful innovators and technically progressive firms', *R & D Management*, Part 7, pp. 191–206.

Rowan, M. (1988) 'Provide a warm welcome', *Micro Decision*, January, pp. 81–4.

Rushton, D. (1986) 'Constructing a database – one firm's experience', *Production Engineer*, December, pp. 17–19.

Scarbrough, H. and Corbett, J. M. (1992) *Technology and Organisation – Power, Meaning and Design*, Routledge, London.

Schill, T. G. and Norback, J. P. (1982) 'Integrating labour data into a computer model', *Food Technology*, Vol. 36, Part 7, pp 72–5.

Selwitz, R. (1991) 'Punching up profits', *Hotel and Motel Management*, 4 February, pp. 37–8.

Senge, P. M. (1990) *The Fifth Discipline, The Art and Practice of the Learning Organisation*, Doubleday, London.

Shamir, B. (1978) 'Between bureaucracy and hospitality', *Journal of Management Studies*, October, pp. 285–307.

Skills and Enterprise Network (1995) *Labour Market and Skills Trends, 1995/6*, Skills and Enterprise Publication, Nottingham, Crown copyright.

Smith, S., Dickson, K. and Woods, A. (1992) '*The industrial divide in services: Technological innovation, co-operation and competition in small employment, design, plant hire firms & garages*', unpublished paper, November.

Snyder, O. P. (1983) 'A computerised flow chart system of food production', *Journal of Food Service Systems*, Vol. 2, Part 4, pp. 211–28.

Stanislao, J. and Stanislao, B. C. (1983) 'Dealing with resistance to change', *Business Horizons*, July/August, pp. 74–8.

Stoner, C. L. (1987) 'Hotel systems pay for themselves', *Hotels and Restaurants International*, August, Vol. 85.

Storey, D. J. (1994) *Understanding the Small Business Sector*, Routledge, London.

Tapscott, D. and Caston, A. (1993) *Paradigm Shift: The New Promise of Information Technology*, McGraw-Hill, New York.

Tarantino, Q. (1994) *Pulp Fiction*, Faber and Faber, London.

Teare, R. and Boer, A. (1991) *Strategic Hospitality Management*, Cassell, London.

Tench, P. (1994) *Fill that bed! Yield management: The technological implications and other effects on four star hotels*, unpublished paper.

Thompson, T. (1988) 'Only connect', *Restaurant Hospitality*, December, pp. 73–8.

Townroe, P. M. (1986) 'Technological change in the service sector: Urban and regional implications', *Technological Change Employment & Spatial Dynamics*, Springer-Verlag, Berlin.

Trist, E.L., Higgin, G. W., Murray, H. and Pollock, A. (1963) *Organizational Choice: Capabilities of groups at the coal face under changing conditions*, Tavistock, London.

Tyler, G. (1991) 'Along the right lines', *Caterer and Hotelkeeper*, 22 August, p. 30.

Umbreit, W. T. (1986) 'Developing behaviourally-anchored scales for evaluating job performance of hotel managers', *International Journal of Hospitality Management*, Vol. 5, No. 2, pp. 55–61.

Whitaker, M. (1986) 'The diffusion of information technology across the hotel and catering industry (UK)', *International Journal of Hospitality Management*, Vol. 5, No. 2, pp. 229–235.

Whitaker, M. (1987) 'Overcoming the barriers to successful implementation of information technology in the UK hotel industry', *International Journal of Hospitality Management*', Vol. 6, No. 4, pp. 229–34.

White, M. (1973) 'Management style in hotels', *HCIMA Journal*, October, pp. 9–11.

Williams, B. (1986) *Attitudes to New Technologies and Economic Growth*, Technical Change Centre, London.

Williams, S. (1987) 'Improving management effectiveness through the use of computer systems in food service operations', *International Journal of Hospitality Management*, Vol. 6, No. 4, pp. 243–5.

Wood, R. C. (1992) *Working in Hotels and Catering*, Routledge, London.

Wood, R. C. (1994) *Organizational Behaviour for Hospitality Management*, Butterworth-Heinemann, Oxford.

Woods, R. H. and Macaulay, J. F. (1989) 'R for turnover: Retention programs that work', *Cornell HRA Quarterly*, Vol. 30, May, pp. 79–90.
Wynne, J. (1994) *The role of the guest in service encounters within luxury hotels*, Edinburgh, paper for CHME research conference.
Zuboff, S. (1988) *In the Age of the Smart Machine: The Future of Work and Power*, Heinemann, Oxford.

INDEX